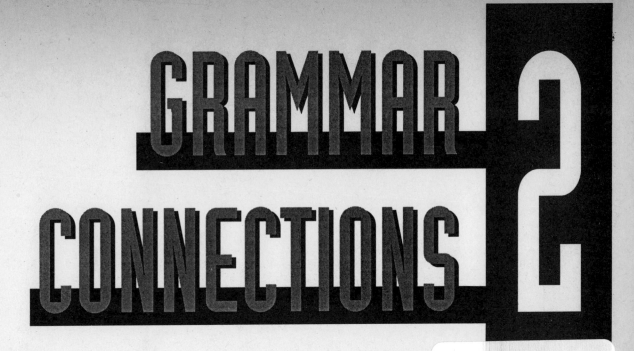

GRAMMAR CONNECTIONS 2

Lynda Berish

Sandra Thibaudeau

with Maria De Rosa Wilson

Prentice Hall Regents Canada, Scarborough, Ontario

CANADIAN CATALOGUING IN PUBLICATION DATA

Berish, Lynda, 1952–
   Grammar connections

ISBN 0-13-310939-9 (v.1)   ISBN 0-13-333288-8 (v.2)

1. English language—Textbooks for second language learners.*
2. English language—Grammar.
I. Thibaudeau, Sandra, 1943–   . II. Title.

PE1128.B47 1994   428.2′4   C94-931523-0

©1996 Prentice-Hall Canada Inc., Scarborough, Ontario

Prentice-Hall, Inc., Englewood Cliffs, New Jersey
Prentice-Hall International, Inc., London
Prentice-Hall of Australia, Pty., Ltd., Sydney
Prentice-Hall of India Pvt., Ltd., New Delhi
Prentice-Hall of Japan, Inc., Tokyo
Prentice-Hall of Southeast Asia (Pte.) Ltd., Singapore
Editora Prentice-Hall do Brasil Ltda., Rio de Janeiro
Prentice-Hall Hispanoamericana, S.A., Mexico

ISBN 0-13-333288-8

Executive editor: Clifford J. Newman
Managing editor: Marta Tomins
Production editor: Elynor Kagan
Production coordinator: Sharon Houston
Design and layout: Joseph Chin
Illustrations: William Kimber
Cover design: Olena Serbyn

Printed and bound in Canada

   3 4 5   99 98 97

To the many students we have had the pleasure of teaching over the years, for the inspiration their many questions have provided.

Contents

Idioms	Conversations	Ten-Minute Grammar Games
to bump into someone to pick someone up to get on to get off to give someone a lift in no time	Do You Want a Lift Sometime?	Solve the Problem Find Out Find Someone
right (here) all right for the time being close to for good to keep your eyes open opens up to grab something	My Neighbourhood	Situations What Are They? Sentence Ends How Much Money?
to miss something/someone at first right away at least to take a walk all the time to be in a hurry to make friends to have fun	A New Country	Solve the Problem Is It True? Times Have Changed A Great Day

Idioms	Conversations	Ten-Minute Grammar Games
to turn (something) on to turn (something) off What's on? for a while to switch over to to be tired of would rather can't stand to make up one's mind guess so/guess not	What's On?	Adjective Options Comparisons What Is It? I Spy
What's the matter? to catch a cold to get/feel/be better, worse by now to take it easy to feel under the weather to come down with something a check-up	Under the Weather	Looking for a Roommate What Is It? Objects and Uses
sharp to go off to get through to one of those things give me a minute to take (something) off never mind	What Happened to You?	What Were They Wearing? Sentence Ends What Was Happening?
a package deal a one-way ticket a return ticket time off to book (tickets) to make (something) out to pick up (something) to talk (something) over to get back to (someone)	A Package Deal	A Quantity Survey What Could It Be? Numbers and Words

Idioms	Conversations	Ten-Minute Grammar Games
to make yourself at home quite a few to introduce yourself to help yourself (to something) to be good at as usual to make a difference	Welcome to the Party	Sentence Ends What Is It? Bumping Words
to look for to have in mind to be at a total loss to look around next door to afford something hold on/hold it to be too good to be true to take one's pick	At the Shopping Mall	Bumping Words Last Session
So far to put something away to get rid of to be in bad shape to fix up (something) at once to be worn out out of the question to make the best of something	Moving In	Puzzles Participles The Old and the New
had better by the way to get in (somewhere) to make it to carry on to fill someone in to go over (something) to take place on the dot	A Meeting	Destinations Future Predictions Solve the Problem

Idioms	Conversations	Ten-Minute Grammar Games
to pick up (something)	Can You Pick Up a Few Things?	Sentence Ends
to be on the run		Chains
to be out of (something)		Sayings and Superstitions
to keep in mind		
to run short of		
to make sure		
to make out (a list)		
to take your time		
to take advantage of		
to stock up on		
Appendix 3 Page 213 Modals for Different Functions	**Appendix 4 Page 214** Special Verb Forms Special Questions	

To the Teacher

Grammar Connections provides a quick review of basic structures and a systematic coverage of elementary and intermediate grammatical structures. It is geared towards students who have a base in English, but who need to complement their language development with attention to accuracy.

The units of the book use a carefully controlled lexicon so as not to detract from the focus on structure. Each one follows a sequence of activities that takes students through several steps.

To begin, new vocabulary is presented visually in a section called "Word Power." This is followed by "Understanding Grammar," a section that includes explanations and comprehensive practice exercises. "Listening and Speaking: Using Idioms" presents the real language that people use every day. The taped dialogues deal with some common difficulties in using social language, and bridge the gap between formal classroom learning and real-life language. Realistic conversations allow students to practise common idiomatic expressions that follow up and build on structures from the units. For example, the formal expression "What are you doing?" is complemented with the idiomatic "What's up?" in the taped dialogues.

Through these three sections, a picture dictionary runs across the bottom of each page to provide an instant reference for new vocabulary. These clear graphic illustrations also support general language development.

The "Ten-Minute Grammar Games" that are included in every unit provide a variety of simple, easy-to-play games and puzzles as a lively way to practise the structures that have been taught. Teachers and students will appreciate activities that involve everyone in a few minutes of fun at the end of a grammar lesson.

Each unit concludes with activities that allow students to test and monitor their own progress. Every fifth unit provides a review of the structures and vocabulary of the preceding four units. Answer keys to all the exercises are included at the back of the book.

1 Present Time

Present Simple Tense
Present Continuous Tense

Present Simple Tense

Affirmative	Negative	Question
I work	I do not	do I
you work	you do not	do you
he works	he does not	does he
she works	she does not	does she
it works	it does not	does it
	work	work?
we work	we do not	do we
you work	you do not	do you
they work	they do not	do they

Present Continuous Tense

Affirmative	Negative	Question
I am	I am not	am I
you are	you are not	are you
he is	he is not	is he
she is	she is not	is she
it is	it is not	is it
working	working	working?
we are	we are not	are we
you are	you are not	are you
they are	they are not	are they

Word Power

People in cities go to work in different ways. Look at the chart and answer the questions.

	Car	Walk	Bus or subway	Average time (minutes)
Grandview	55%	25%	20%	38
Midland	45%	25%	30%	45
Riverside	55%	15%	30%	55
Eastlake	60%	30%	10%	15
Cedarcrest	25%	30%	45%	35
Hamilton	30%	40%	30%	40
Trenton	60%	10%	30%	55
Darby	45%	10%	45%	45
York	30%	25%	45%	30
Greensberg	20%	30%	50%	60

Susan (Eastlake) **Bill (Darby)** **Michael (Greensberg)** **Steve (Trenton)** **Maria (Hamilton)**

Fred (Grandview) **Tom (Riverside)** **Vera (Midland)** **Lee (Cedarcrest)** **Kim (York)**

Read the sentences and write **T** (true) or **F** (false). Correct information that is false.

1. It takes Maria 40 minutes to get to work.
2. Vera probably drives to work.
3. Susan doesn't have a car. She probably walks to work.
4. Steve probably walks to work.
5. Kim probably takes public transportation to work.
6. It takes Lee 20 minutes to go to work.
7. Fred probably takes the subway to go to work.
8. Tom most likely walks to work.
9. It takes Michael an hour to get to work.
10. Bill probably drives or takes public transportation to work.

Understanding Grammar

UNDERSTAND: **Present Simple Tense**

Use the present simple tense to describe habitual actions or things in nature that don't change.

> I take a bus to work.
> The sun rises in the east.

Affirmative

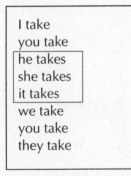

I take
you take
he takes
she takes
it takes
we take
you take
they take

> **TEACHER'S BOX:** Use **es** as the 3rd person singular ending when a verb ends in **ch**, **sh**, **x**, **ss**, or **o**. Examples are **watches**, **fixes**, **goes**. Pronounce the ending /**z**/.

Use the base form of the verb for the present simple tense. Add **s** or **es** to the base form of the verb with **he**, **she**, or **it**.

> I take the bus.
> **She goes** by car.

| a bus | a subway | to drive | to walk | to work |

4

Read the paragraph that Karen wrote. Answer the questions that follow. Correct the information where necessary.

Do people all go to work in the city in the same way?

No, they go to work in different ways.

There are many big cities in the world. People go to work in the city in different ways. When the sun rises in the east, people in big cities usually wake up early and get ready for the day. People go to their jobs or classes by different means of transportation. My neighbour works downtown. He goes to work by car. I don't like to drive at rush hour so I usually walk a few blocks to the bus stop. Then I take the bus to work. A student lives in the apartment next door. She rides her bicycle in spring, summer, and fall. She goes to class by subway in winter.

1. Does the sun rise in the west?
2. Do people in big cities usually wake up early?
3. Do all the people who work downtown go by bus?
4. Does the neighbour walk to work?
5. Does Karen ride a bicycle to the bus stop?
6. Does Karen drive a car to work?
7. Does Karen get the bus in front of her house?
8. Does the student live in a house?
9. Does the student usually ride her bicycle to class?
10. Does the student ride her bicycle in the winter?

Negative

Add **do not** before the base form of the main verb to make the negative form.

I do not know.

When the subject is **he**, **she**, or **it**, use **does not** before the base form of the main verb. For the negative form of the 3rd person singular, do not add **s** or **es** to the main verb. Add it to the auxiliary verb **do** (**does**):

✔ He **does** not **know**.

✘ He **does** not **knows**.

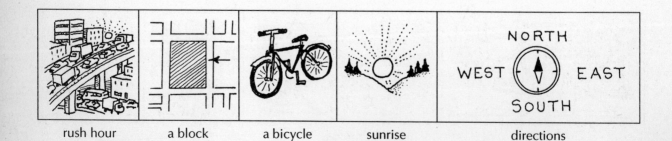

rush hour   a block   a bicycle   sunrise   directions

<table>
<tr><td>

Negative

I do not
you do not
he does not
she does not
it does not

we do not
you do not
they do not

work

</td><td>

Negative Contraction

I don't
you don't
he doesn't
she doesn't
it doesn't

work

we don't
you don't
they don't

</td><td>

Language in Transition

The full form of the simple present negative uses the negative form **do not** or **does not**. It is used mainly for formal writing or for emphasis. In spoken English and informal written English the contraction (**don't** or **doesn't**) is generally used.

</td></tr>
</table>

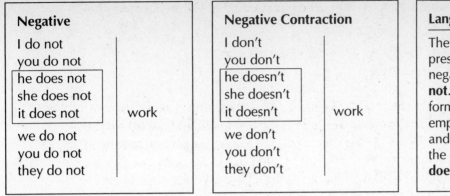

Change the statements to the negative form. Use contractions.

1. In the summer I drive to work.
2. It takes a long time to get downtown.
3. The subway opens at six o'clock.
4. Mei and Karen leave for work at the same time.
5. Vancouver and Kyoto have subway systems.
6. Bob goes to work by public transportation.
7. Miguel likes to walk to work.
8. Suzanne and Tania live in the same building.
9. The bus leaves at exactly 8:15.
10. Mike rides his bike to class in the winter.

Question

To ask a question in the simple present tense, use **do** or **does** before the subject. Put a question mark (**?**) at the end of the sentence.

Do you take the bus to work?

Does she walk to work?

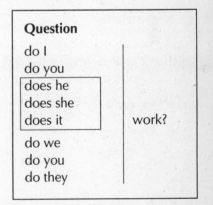

Question	
do I	
do you	
does he	
does she	
does it	work?
do we	
do you	
do they	

winter   summer   to leave   to live

6

Some sentences have errors. Find the errors and correct them.

1. Do he walk to work?
2. Does she drive to work?
3. Does they take the bus often?
4. Do they have a new car?
5. Does the bus sometimes come late?
6. Do they likes the subway?
7. Does she drives to work?
8. Do you takes the bus?
9. Does she needs a car?
10. Do they rides their bicycles to class?

UNDERSTAND: **Present Continuous Tense**

The continuous aspect describes how an action takes place. It focuses on the moment that something is happening.

Use the present continuous for actions that are in progress now:

I am standing at the bus stop.

Use the present continuous for temporary situations:

They are travelling in South America at the moment.

To form the present continuous, put the auxiliary verb **be** before the main verb. Add **ing** to the main verb. Note that the ending **ing** shows continuous action. The auxiliary verb (**am**, **is**, or **are**) shows present time.

TEACHER'S BOX: For rules on spelling the present continuous, see Appendix 1, page 209.

Affirmative		Contraction	
I am		I'm	
you are		you're	
he is		he's	
she is		she's	
it is	standing	it's	standing
we are		we're	
you are		you're	
they are		they're	

to travel   a newspaper   an egg   toast   to cook   a package

A. Complete the paragraph by choosing the best verb for each space. Put the verbs in the present continuous form.

wait   cook   read   stand   have   sit   pour   make   hold   put

This is a picture of Mother's Day at my house. My mother _____ at the table. She _____ the newspaper. My father is at the stove. He _____ some eggs. My younger sister _____ flowers on the table. They are a surprise for mother. My older brother _____ at the counter. He _____ coffee into two mugs. I am at the counter too. I _____ toast. I _____ for the toast to be ready. My older sister _____ a package. It is a Mother's Day present. We _____ a good time.

TEACHER'S BOX: The dynamic use of **have** is not necessarily carried over into other languages. It may be useful to draw students' attention to such expressions as **have a good time**, **have a bath**, **have breakfast**, **have a coffee**, **have a baby**.

The continuous aspect describes how actions take place. Some verbs describe a state, not an action. These verbs cannot have continuous aspect.

to pour   to make   to hold   a stove   a counter   a mug

B. Which verbs describe actions?

know	hear	like	walk
take	look at	love	speak
study	want	listen	need
learn	eat	seem	give
believe	sit	own	read

C. Write a sentence with the present continuous form of the action verbs from the list. Use different subject pronouns to begin your sentences.

I am taking an English course at the moment.

Negative

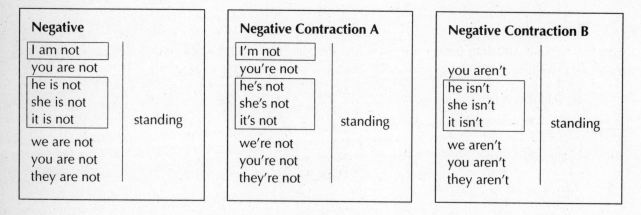

Negative	
I am not	
you are not	
he is not	
she is not	
it is not	standing
we are not	
you are not	
they are not	

Negative Contraction A	
I'm not	
you're not	
he's not	
she's not	
it's not	standing
we're not	
you're not	
they're not	

Negative Contraction B	
you aren't	
he isn't	
she isn't	
it isn't	standing
we aren't	
you aren't	
they aren't	

Use **not** after the auxiliary verb **be**. Use the **ing** form of the main verb to show continuous action. The auxiliary verb (**am**, **is**, or **are**) shows that the action is in present time. Use the auxiliary verb **be** to form negation.

I **am not standing** in the right line.

Language in Transition

The full form of the present continuous negative uses **am not**, **is not**, or **are not** followed by the base form of the main verb (see chart on page 1). The full form is used for formal writing or for emphasis. The contraction is used for spoken English and informal written English. There are two ways to form the contraction:

He **isn't** standing in the right line.
He**'s not** standing in the right line.

| to stand | to know | to want | to own | to like | to love |

Make these sentences negative. Use the form of Contraction B.

1. Ray is taking the bus today.
2. The sun is shining this morning.
3. They are listening to music in the living room
4. Maurice is learning to speak Japanese.
5. My neighbours are travelling in South America.
6. The students are writing an exam now.
7. Yumi is giving Max a birthday gift.
8. It is raining hard right now.
9. She is reading an exciting novel in her English class.
10. They are watching a movie on the TV.

Question

Use the auxiliary verb to form questions. Put the auxiliary verb **be** before the subject. The main verb uses the **ing** form. Put a question mark (**?**) at the end of the sentence.

Are you waiting for me?

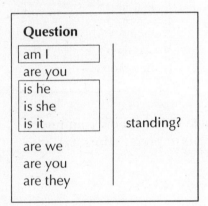

Some sentences have errors. Find the errors and correct them.

1. Is the bus taking a long time this morning?
2. Are you taking the same bus, Nick?
3. Is Tom take his bicycle today?
4. Are they leaving their car at home?
5. Are you wait for me?
6. Is she look at us?
7. Are you talking to me?
8. Are you wait for the bus?
9. Is the man read a newspaper?
10. Is Lena carrying a briefcase?

| to learn | to take | a gift | to look at | to wait for | a briefcase |

UNDERSTAND: **Present Simple and Present Continuous in Contrast**

Use the present simple tense to describe habitual actions (**He goes to work every day**) or things in nature or life that don't change (**Tigers eat meat**).

Use the continuous aspect to describe actions that take place as we speak (**He is sitting over there**) or that we know about at the time they happen (**They are having a math exam today**).

A. Look at the pictures and choose the correct form of the verb.

Susan _____ (work) downtown. Usually she _____ (drive) her car to work. This morning she is in the subway. She _____ (look) at her watch. She _____ (like) to arrive for work on time.

Tony usually _____ (walk) to work. Today he _____ (take) the bus. A lot of people _____ (stand) at the bus stop. It _____ (rain). People _____ (hold) up their umbrellas. Tony _____ (want) to go home and sleep.

B. Some sentences have tenses that are wrong. Correct the errors.

1. My friend takes the bus to work.
2. He is walking to the bus stop every day.
3. He usually meets his neighbours at the bus stop.
4. They are liking to talk about sports.
5. This morning they are talking about the hockey game.
6. That person isn't talking with them.
7. He often is bringing a newspaper to read.
8. He is liking to sit on a bench and read.
9. Today he reads the comics.
10. The comics are funny. He is smiling.

| a watch | a bench | to rain | an umbrella | to sleep | a hockey game |

Listening and Speaking: Using Idioms

Do You Want a Lift Sometime?

A. Study the expressions used in the sentences.

1. If you want to go downtown, you **get on** the bus at the corner.
2. **Get off** the bus at the end of the line.
3. Yesterday I was shopping, and I **bumped into** an old friend.
4. I usually drive to work. Do you want **a lift** sometime?
5. I can give you a lift tomorrow. What time should I **pick** you **up**?
6. The bus is slow, but if we drive, we can be there **in no time**.

B. Match the expressions to the meanings. Use the sentences above to help you.

1. to get on
2. to get off
3. to bump into
4. to give a lift
5. to pick someone up
6. in no time

a) to meet by accident
b) very soon
c) to give someone a ride in a car
d) to get someone and give them a ride
e) to enter a vehicle
f) to leave a vehicle

C. Listen and answer the questions.

1. How do Nancy and Ana come to class?
2. What does Nancy do at Berry Street?
3. How does Ana sometimes come to class?
4. Where can she pick Nancy up?

Turn to page 15 for Exercise D.

to get on   to get off   to bump into   vehicles   at the corner   to shop

Ten-Minute Grammar Games

Solve the Problem

Focus: Review present tense verbs.

Students work in pairs to find the profession of each woman. When they have finished, they can check the answer in the answer key (page 225).

Three young women, Michiko, Maria, and Gaby, live next door to each other in an apartment building. Maria lives between her two friends. They work as a model, a decorator, and a journalist. The decorator walks Gaby's dog when she goes on holiday. The journalist taps on Michiko's wall when her TV is too loud.

Name	Profession
Michiko	
Maria	
Gaby	

Find Out

Focus: Present tense verbs, question form.

Students work in pairs or small groups to brainstorm a list of questions in the present simple tense on the topics listed below.

food
sports
entertainment
hobbies
work
family
clothes
travel

What is your favourite food?

How many sisters do you have?

Students use their questions to interview two students from another group. Then they present the information to the class.

Find Someone

Focus: Practise questions and answers with present simple and present continuous verbs.

The aim is for students to find at least one person who fits each description on the list. Students walk around the room asking each other questions. When a person answers "yes," his or her name is written beside the description on the list. The first person to finish is the winner. Students in the class can be asked to confirm or deny the information as the winner reads it out.

Find someone who…

1. has one sister and one brother.
2. has a motorcycle.
3. is wearing blue socks today.
4. is using a red pen right now.
5. is wearing earrings.
6. has a pet dog.
7. speaks three languages.
8. drinks coffee in the evening.
9. prepares his or her own lunch every day.
10. plays a musical instrument.
11. is wearing blue jeans today.
12. is wearing a belt.
13. is wearing a necklace.
14. likes to ski.

Test Yourself

Present Time

A. Read the paragraphs and answer the questions with complete sentences.

Karen is a receptionist in an office downtown. She usually leaves for work early because she likes to arrive early. When she is late, she doesn't have time to drink coffee and read the paper before she starts her job. Karen begins work at nine o'clock.

Other people in Karen's office have coffee at home and arrive later. Fred sometimes arrives in a bad mood because he has trouble finding a place to park his car. He often has to park several blocks away and walk to the office. Karen is happy that she lives near the subway and that she doesn't need to worry about parking. Maxine and Lili live near the office so they can walk to work.

1. Where does Karen work?
2. Why does she usually leave for work early?
3. When doesn't she have time for coffee?
4. When does she like to read the newspaper?
5. What time does Karen begin work?
6. Why does Fred sometimes arrive in a bad mood?
7. Where does he often have to park?
8. Where does Karen live?
9. Why is Karen happy about where she lives?
10. How do Maxine and Lili come to work?

B. Choose the present simple or the present continuous.

1. a) He is running for the train every day.
   b) He runs for the train every day.

2. a) She likes to take the subway to work.
   b) She is liking to take the subway to work.

3. a) The students are walking to class every day.
   b) The students walk to class every day.

4. a) They go to the swimming pool every summer.
   b) They are going to the swimming pool every summer.

5. a) My sister is working at the bank downtown this week.
   b) My sister works at the bank downtown this week.

6. a) The children get ready for school now.
   b) The children are getting ready for school now.

7. a) Please open the door; the doorbell is ringing.
   b) Please open the door; the doorbell rings.

8. a) People are usually standing in line at bus stops.
   b) People usually stand in line at bus stops.

9. a) They are not home now because they are travelling in Europe.
   b) They are not home now because they travel in Europe.

10. a) I'm liking my new job with the bus company.
    b) I like my new job with the bus company.

Questions

Write a question for each sentence. Use the question words to help you.

1. Min works in a cafe as a cook. (Where)
2. She works on Fridays and Saturdays. (When)
3. She likes her job because it is interesting. (Why)
4. Today she is working behind the counter. (Where)
5. She is making sandwiches for the customers. (What)
6. When the sandwiches are ready she calls the server. (Who)
7. The server carries the sandwiches to the tables. (Where)
8. One customer is ordering coffee. (What)
9. Min is making the coffee in the kitchen. (Where)
10. Min and the server are tired because the restaurant is busy. (Why)

Negative

Write these sentences in the negative form. Use contractions.

1. The bus company has 50 buses on the road.
2. The buses serve all the people in the city.
3. Tony drives a bus on the weekends.
4. Tony is working for the bus company at the moment.
5. He wants to drive a bus all his life.
6. Susanna is learning Tony's route.
7. She wants to work during the week.
8. They like to work at night.
9. The bus company asks her to work on Sundays.
10. Susanna is thinking about getting a new job.

Idioms

Use the correct form of these expressions to complete the paragraph.

to bump into someone	to get off
to pick someone up	to give someone a lift
to get on	in no time

I take the bus to work almost every day. I _____ the bus at the corner of my street. My neighbour, Kathy, sometimes takes the bus too. She also works downtown. Sometimes we _____ each other at the bus stop. My friend Joe often _____ the bus there too. He works at a hospital, so he _____ at the bus stop near the front door of the hospital.

On some mornings there isn't much traffic, and we get downtown _____. We _____ the bus near our offices. Kathy sometimes drives to work, so she _____ me a _____. She _____ me _____ at my house, and we drive down together. Then Kathy parks her car in the parking lot behind her building. Kathy works with two people who live in our neighbourhood. When she _____ them in the corridor, she offers to _____ them a _____ home.

Score for Test Yourself: _____
50

Listening and Speaking: Using Idioms

Do You Want a Lift Sometime?

D. Listen to the conversation. Write the missing words.

Ana: How do you usually come to class, Nancy?

Nancy: I take the bus. How about you, Ana?

Ana: I usually take the bus too. Which bus do you take?

Nancy: I take the 49 to Berry Street. I get off at Berry Street, and get on the 103. That takes me right downtown.

Ana: Oh. I take the 56. I also get _____ at Berry Street and _____ on the 103.

Nancy: Really? Well, maybe we'll bump _____ each other some time on the bus.

Ana: Sure. Anything's possible. Sometimes I drive to work though. Do you want a _____ some time?

Nancy: That would be great. If you pick me _____ at the bus stop, we can get downtown in _____ time.

E. Practise the conversation with a partner.

F. Work with a partner. Write a conversation about how you come to class. Use as many expressions as you can.

2 Articles
Indefinite
Definite

Indefinite article	Type of noun	Example
Count		
a	singular count before consonant **sounds**	a tree, a university
an	singular count before vowel **sounds**	an apple, an hour
0 article	plural count	trees, universities
		apples, hours
some	indefinite quantity plural count	some trees, some universities
		some apples, some hours
Non-count		
0 article	non-count	grass (in general): "Grass is green."
some	indefinite quantity non-count	some grass: "Some grass is yellow."

Word Power

Look at the picture of a neighbourhood. Find the following:

**a drug store   a fence   a fire hydrant   a hospital   neighbours   an ambulance   children
grass   a letter carrier   a hardware store   a bench   a bus stop   flowers   a water fountain
a truck   a traffic light   a university   a cross walk**

Understanding Grammar

UNDERSTAND: **Indefinite Articles**

Indefinite article	Type of noun	Example
Count		
a	singular count before consonant **sounds**	a tree, a university
an	singular count before vowel **sounds**	an apple, an hour
0 article	plural count	trees, universities
		apples, hours
some	indefinite quantity plural count	some trees, some universities
		some apples, some hours
Non-count		
0 article	non-count	grass (in general): "Grass is green."
some	indefinite quantity non-count	some grass: "Some grass is yellow."

Indefinite articles are used to identify or classify people or things **in general**.

Singular Count Nouns

To identify a person or thing (singular), use the indefinite article before count nouns. Use **a** if nouns begin with consonant sounds. Use **an** if nouns begin with vowel sounds.

She's a doctor.

It's an ambulance.

> **TEACHER'S BOX:** It is the **sound** rather that the presence of a vowel or a consonant that determines the use of **a** or **an**: **a one-way street**, **an honest man**.

To refer to quantity (singular), use the indefinite article **a/an**.

I need a dictionary. (one)

I need an orderly. (one)

> **TEACHER'S BOX:** It is incorrect to use **one** in place of **a/an** unless you specifically wish to distinguish **one** from another number: **I bought one dictionary, not three**.

a doctor   an orderly   an ambulance   grass   a tree   an apple

20

Write **a** or **an** before the noun. Say the words and listen for the sound.

1. ____ hospital
2. ____ hour
3. ____ ambulance
4. ____ hardware store
5. ____ bench
6. ____ store
7. ____ university
8. ____ fire hydrant
9. ____ police officer
10. ____ opera singer

11. ____ honest man
12. ____ neighbour
13. ____ accident
14. ____ garden
15. ____ avenue
16. ____ street
17. ____ open window
18. ____ elevator
19. ____ indoor pool
20. ____ umbrella

Plural Count Nouns

To classify or identify people or things (plural) use **0 article**.

Books are useful.

Read the descriptions. What are these things?

1. They take you from one place to another. They have a sign on top. They are useful if you are in a hurry or have heavy packages. They can be expensive.

2. They are often on the corner of streets. They are made of metal and are shorter than a person. They have a slot to put things inside.

3. You have to look up to see the tops. You can't find them in small towns. People have to take elevators to go to the offices inside them. They are glass or steel.

4. They have three colours that change. They can be on a post or in the air above an intersection. Sometimes they have simple pictures on them and sometimes they flash.

5. You find them in towns and cities. They keep you safe. They are found at intersections. They are striped, and go from one side of the street to the other.

6. These are good places to relax or to get information. You have to speak quietly when you are in them. Some people read there. Other people study. Some people even sleep.

7. They have many cars and help people get around the city quickly. You need tickets, change, or a pass to ride on them. They make a lot of noise when they pull into a station underground.

8. They are a fast way to go somewhere for help if you are sick or hurt. They can travel very quickly because other cars let them pass when they hear their sirens.

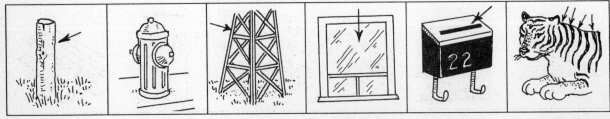

a post   a fire hydrant   steel   glass   a slot   stripes

9. They are always open and they are usually very big. They have many rooms and many beds, but people don't usually like to stay there for very long. Sometimes people have to stay there if they are sick or hurt.

10. These are good places to relax or to get exercise. There are benches, water fountains, trees, flowers, and picnic tables. They have many green spaces and small animals may live there.

Note: If you have trouble, see the words on page 30 for help.

> **TEACHER'S BOX:** Adjectives are always singular in English. They do not agree in number with the nouns they modify.
>
> ✗ They have bigs cars   ✔ They have big cars.

Indefinite Quantities

To refer to an indefinite (plural) quantity with count nouns, use **some**.

  She likes oranges. (in general)

  She bought some oranges. (indefinite quantity)

To refer to an indefinite quantity with non-count nouns, use **some**.

  He likes butter. (in general)

  He bought some butter. (indefinite quantity)

Choose **some** or 0 article.

1. _____ flowers smell nice.
2. _____ ice is cold.
3. _____ grass is green.
4. _____ fish swim.
5. _____ neighbours are friendly.
6. _____ fire trucks are yellow.
7. _____ cats don't like water.
8. _____ buses are air-conditioned.

9. _____ parties are fun.
10. _____ students work hard.
11. _____ sugar is white.
12. _____ candy is sweet.
13. _____ cities are dirty.
14. _____ children are noisy.
15. _____ tropical countries are hot.
16. _____ men are handsome.

to flash   a skyscraper   a ticket   a sign   a water fountain   a picnic table

Non-count Nouns

Don't use **a/an** before non-count nouns. Use 0 article.

- ✔ It's butter.   ✘ It's a butter.
- ✔ Sugar is sweet.   ✘ A sugar is sweet.

Make a list of count nouns and a list of non-count nouns. Use the indefinite article **a/an** before the count nouns. Use **0 article** before the non-count nouns.

water	car	fire fighter
flower	gas	letter carrier
air	telephone	mail
store	neighbour	fun
hospital	fence	sunshine
garbage	ambulance	park
orderly	police	child

UNDERSTAND: **Definite Articles**

Definite articles are used for **specific** references. Use definite articles if you can answer the question "Which?"

1. Use the definite article **the** when the speaker and listener know which person or thing they are talking about because:

   a) The person or thing was mentioned before.

   > I took a picture of a child. **The** child was my son.

   b) The person or thing is specified by a phrase.

   > **the** University **of** Toronto
   > **the** best show **in** town
   > **the** movie **that** you saw yesterday

   c) The speakers share the same context or knowledge.

   > The library is open today. (the library **in our college**)
   > The coffee is good. (the coffee **in this restaurant**)

2. Use the definite article when you are talking about something **unique**.

   > The moon is a crescent tonight.
   > The Amazon is a river in South America.

a fence   gas   the moon   a crescent   a river   garbage

Use **the** before singular or plural count nouns and before non-count nouns:

the neighbour
the neighbours
the water

> **TEACHER'S BOX:** Suggest to students that they remember to use **the** only if they can answer the question **Which?**

A. Read the sentences. Add information that makes the nouns specific.

He is the king **of Morocco**.
I met the students **from our class**.
The child **with long hair** is my cousin.

1. The children _____ are my cousins.
2. We picked the flowers _____.
3. The water _____ is cold.
4. The hospital _____ is very big.
5. Andy knows the man _____.
6. The restaurant _____ served excellent food.
7. The book _____ is interesting.
8. We go to the park _____ often.
9. The car _____ is mine.
10. The coffee _____ is Brazilian.

> **TEACHER'S BOX:** **The** indicates that the noun is definite. It may help students to understand the notion of definite reference if a prepositional phrase (**with blue eyes, on the corner, of Morocco**) or a relative clause (**who is wearing glasses, where we met yesterday**) is used to make the noun more specific.

B. Put the definite article **the** before nouns that refer to specific people or things. Put a **0** sign before nouns that are general.

0 neighbours are people who live near you.
The neighbours in our apartment building are friendly.

1. I like _____ sugar in my tea.
2. _____ letter carriers wear uniforms.
3. We want to invite _____ neighbours to our party.
4. _____ city streets usually have sidewalks.

flowers   to pick   long hair   a king   a sidewalk   tea

5. _____ bicycles outside are not ours.
6. _____ moon will be full tonight.
7. They want to paint _____ fence white.
8. _____ weather today is very cold.
9. People like to sit on _____ park benches.
10. We took a picture of _____ Rocky Mountains.
11. We will buy our tickets at _____ airport.
12. _____ people shop in big supermarkets.
13. A lot of cities have _____ skyscrapers.
14. I hear that _____ food in that restaurant is excellent.
15. Hollywood is famous for _____ movies that are made there.

Listening and Speaking: Using Idioms

My Neighbourhood

A. Find the correct meaning for each idiom.

1. I live **right** on the corner of Pine and Yates.
   a) approximately   b) exactly

2. This job is not very interesting, but it's **all right**.
   a) acceptable   b) unacceptable

3. This apartment is small, but I'll stay here **for the time being**.
   a) for a long time   b) for now

4. I live **close to** the bus stop.
   a) near   b) far

5. Are you planning to live in this house **for good**, or will you move next year?
   a) permanently   b) temporarily

6. It's very busy downtown today. **Keep your eyes open** for a parking space.
   a) stay awake   b) look for

7. I need a large apartment. I hope something **opens up** soon.
   a) gets bigger   b) becomes available

8. If you see a nice shirt on sale you should **grab it**.
   a) try it on   b) buy it

full moon   to paint   Rocky Mountains   a picture   a parking space   a shirt

B. Listen and answer the questions.

    1. Where does Mario live?
    2. What does Mario like about his apartment for the time being?
    3. What does Mario not like about his apartment?
    4. What is Carlos looking for?

Turn to page 29 for Exercise C.

Ten-Minute Grammar Games

Situations

Focus: Practise indefinite and definite articles.

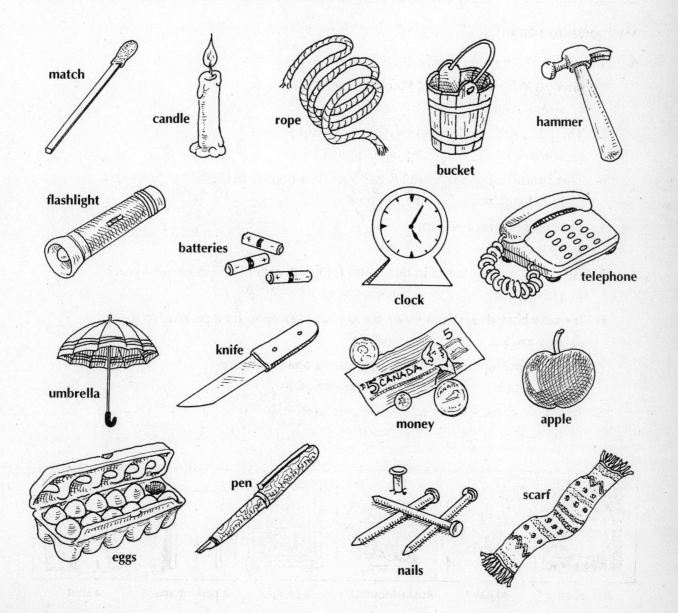

match

candle

rope

bucket

hammer

flashlight

batteries

clock

telephone

umbrella

knife

money

apple

eggs

pen

nails

scarf

1. Students work in groups. They choose one of the following situations, and make a list of the items they can use, inserting an indication of the quantity they need (some money, a rope):

   a fire

   an electrical storm

   a snowstorm

   a flood

2. Together, students write a paragraph describing how they would use the items.

   In a fire, I can use the rope to climb out of a window. I can eat an apple when I am hungry.

What Are They?

Focus: Review vocabulary, practise indefinite articles.

Work with a partner. Complete the crossword puzzle, using the clues below.

Across

2. some young people in a family
6. some things that smell nice
8. something you need in order to breathe
9. a place to cross a street safely
12. a person who lives next door to you
14. a place for higher education
15. a person who helps sick or hurt people
18. a vehicle that takes you to the hospital
19. a place to grow flowers in front of your house

Down

1. a place you go to buy things
3. a place you go when you are sick or hurt
4. a place you go to buy lunch or supper
5. a very tall office building
7. a store where you can buy a hammer and nails
10. something you use outside when it rains
11. a car that you hire to drive you somewhere
13. a book you use to find the meaning of a word
16. a place you go to relax outside
17. an object you use to call another person
19. something you put in your car to make it go

Sentences Ends

Focus: Practise indefinite and definite articles.

Students complete these sentences alone. Then they work in groups to talk about their answers. They can ask each other questions to find out more about their choices.

1. The most useful thing I own is …
2. Some things I want to buy are …
3. The thing I am most afraid of is …
4. My favourite thing to wear is …
5. A good gift for a friend is …
6. Some good foods to serve at a party are …

How Much Money?

Focus: Practise definite and indefinite articles.

Students work in groups. They are told to imagine that they are in a large department store. They have the following amounts of money, and a ten-minute time limit to spend each amount. They use their imaginations to think of the most interesting things possible to buy for each amount. The group with the most imaginative list wins.

$15 $50 $100 $250 $500 $1,000

With $15, we could buy some gum, a novel, a T-shirt, etc.

Test Yourself

Indefinite Articles

A.   Choose the correct form of the indefinite article: **a/an** or **some**.

A New House

Tom and Louise are moving to _____ new house. They need many things for their kitchen. They need _____ stove with _____ oven. They also need _____ refrigerator and _____ washing machine. Tom wants _____ table and _____ folding chairs.

Louise and Tom love their back yard. They need many things there too. They need _____ table, _____ chairs, and _____ umbrella for the patio. Louise wants to plant _____ vegetables near the fence. She wants to plant _____ tomatoes and _____ carrots. Tom likes fruit trees. He wants to have _____ apple tree in the yard.

Louise and Tom have children. They have _____ young girl and _____ older boy. The children have _____ pets. They have _____ small cat, _____ enormous dog, and _____ fish. They are happy because there is _____ big yard to play in. They want to meet _____ children from the neighbourhood and play in the back yard.

B.   Choose **some** or **0** article to complete the sentences.

1.   _____ apples are red.
2.   _____ oranges are orange.
3.   _____ rice is brown.
4.   _____ snow is cold.
5.   _____ water is wet.
6.   _____ water is cold.
7.   _____ teachers are women.
8.   _____ cars are expensive.
9.   _____ cities are crowded.
10.   _____ fire is hot.

Definite Articles

Some sentences have errors. Find the errors and correct them.

1. Temperature in this city can be very high.
2. Many people in North America have the pets.
3. People sometimes park on the street at night.
4. Most households have the telephones.
5. You can report stolen cars to the police.
6. Police station is down the street.
7. A lot of people in Vancouver work in the offices.
8. Traffic lights at the corner are not working.
9. The climate here is very hot.
10. Climates vary from one city to another.

Idioms

Replace the boldface words with appropriate expressions. Use the correct form of these expressions to help you.

right	for good
all right	to keep your eyes open
for the time being	opens up
close to	to grab something

1. I want to buy a used car. If I see a good one, at a reasonable price, I'll **buy it immediately**.
2. My job is boring, but it's okay **for now**.
3. I work downtown. My office is **near** the subway.
4. This coat is not very warm. It's **okay** for the fall, but it isn't warm enough for the winter.
5. I'm looking for a new job. If a new job **becomes available** in your office, please let me know.
6. I just bought a beautiful new house. I don't want to move for a long time. I want to stay here **permanently**.
7. Susan **was watchful and alert**, and found a great apartment **exactly** downtown.

Score for Test Yourself: _____
50

⊙⊙ Listening and Speaking: Using Idioms

My Neighbourhood

C. Listen and write the missing words.

Carlos: Where do you live, Mario?

Mario: I live _____ downtown, Carlos.

Carlos: Do you like it?

Mario: Yeah, it's all _____ for the time _____, because it's close _____ my work.

Carlos: That sounds good.

Mario: It is. But there's a lot of traffic on my street, and it's noisy. It's okay for now, but I'm not staying here for _____.

Carlos: I understand. I live in a busy part of town too, but I'm keeping my eyes _____ for a place in a quieter neighbourhood. If something good opens _____, I'll grab _____.

Mario: Well, good luck.

Carlos: You too.

D. Practise the conversation with a partner.

E. Write a conversation about where you live. Use as many expressions as you can.

Plural count nouns for page 21

taxis, libraries, cross walks, parks, subways, ambulances, traffic lights, hospitals, skyscrapers, mailboxes

3

Simple Past Tense Regular
Simple Past Tense Irregular
"Used to" for Past Habits

Simple Past Tense Regular

Affirmative

I worked
you worked
he worked
she worked
it worked

we worked
you worked
they worked

Negative

I did not	
you did not	
he did not	
she did not	work
it did not	
we did not	
you did not	
they did not	

Negative Contraction

I didn't	
you didn't	
he didn't	
she didn't	work
it didn't	
we didn't	
you didn't	
they didn't	

Question

did I	
did you	
did he	
did she	work?
did it	
did we	
did you	
did they	

Simple Past Tense Irregular

Base form	Irregular form of simple past affirmative	Base form	Irregular form of simple past affirmative
be	was/were	lay	laid
beat	beat	lead	led
become	became	let	let
begin	began	leave	left
bite	bit	lie	lay
bleed	bled	lose	lost
blow	blew	make	made
break	broke	mean	meant
bring	brought	meet	met
build	built	pay	paid
buy	bought	put	put
catch	caught	read	read (/red/)
choose	chose	ride	rode
come	came	ring	rang
cost	cost	rise	rose
cut	cut	run	ran
dig	dug	see	saw
do	did	sell	sold
draw	drew	send	sent
drink	drank	shake	shook
drive	drove	shine	shone
eat	ate	shoot	shot
fall	fell	shrink	shrank
feed	fed	shut	shut
feel	felt	sing	sang
fly	flew	sit	sat
find	found	sleep	slept
forget	forgot	spread	spread
forgive	forgave	speak	spoke
freeze	froze	stand	stood
get	got	steal	stole
give	gave	swim	swam
go	went	take	took
grow	grew	teach	taught
have	had	tell	told
hear	heard	think	thought
hide	hid	throw	threw
hit	hit	understand	understood
hold	held	wake	woke
hurt	hurt	wear	wore
keep	kept	win	won
know	knew	write	wrote

Word Power

Work with a partner. Describe the things you see in the pictures.

Understanding Grammar

UNDERSTAND: **Simple Past Tense**

Use the simple past tense for actions **completed** in past time.

I watched a movie last night.

TEACHER'S BOX: Because the simple past tense is used for action that began and ended in past time, it is important that a marker of past time be used or be understood by the context: **I studied hard last night. I studied hard for the exam (before the exam).**

The regular form of the simple past tense is formed by adding **ed** to the base form of the verb.

I walk   I walk**ed**

Some verbs require spelling changes before the ed is added. See the chart in Appendix 1, page 209.

Many common everyday verbs are irregular in the affirmative form of the simple past tense. See the chart in Appendix 2, page 211.

A. Match the base form with the past tense affirmative form.

1. live	a) told
2. take	b) climbed
3. eat	c) ran
4. run	d) gave
5. climb	e) saw
6. throw	f) went
7. meet	g) threw
8. go	h) found
9. bring	i) got
10. put	j) put
11. give	k) brought
12. say	l) lived
13. know	m) ate
14. tell	n) came
15. come	o) took
16. find	p) met
17. see	q) knew
18. get	r) said

to climb   to throw   to run   to bring   to give   to put

B. Read the story. Put the verbs in the simple past tense.

The Apple Tree

When we were young, we _____ (live) in the country. My brother and I _____ (go) to school together every day. We often _____ (meet) our friends along the road. We usually _____ (take) our time. We _____ (hunt) rabbits and looked for fruit trees. The road to the school _____ (run) past farmers' fields.

One fall day we _____ (get) into trouble with a farmer. We _____ (find) an apple tree. When we _____ (see) the juicy red apples, my friend _____ (climb) the tree. He picked apples and _____ (throw) them down. I _____ (catch) the apples and we all _____ (eat) a lot. The farmer _____ (see) us eating his apples and was very angry.

We _____ (bring) a nice red apple to the teacher at school. My brother _____ (put) the apple on the teacher's desk. When the teacher _____ (see) the apple, she said, "Thank you." Nobody _____ (tell) her where the apple _____ (come) from.

to hunt   a rabbit   a field   to pick   to throw   to catch

C. Choose the verbs to complete the sentences. Write the verbs in the simple past tense.

eat   bring   come   tell   know   put   take   run   meet   throw

1. Alex often _____ to class late.
2. We all _____ our school bags to class.
3. Jenna _____ her books on her desk.
4. Sometimes Michel _____ his coat on the floor.
5. We usually _____ lunch in the classroom.
6. After class we _____ our friends outside.
7. The teacher _____ us about our homework.
8. We _____ that there was a math test every Thursday.
9. It _____ a long time to finish the math test.
10. We _____ home when school finished.

UNDERSTAND: **Simple Past Tense Negative Form**

Regular and irregular past tense verbs form the negative in the same way. The auxiliary verb **did** signals past time and **not** signals negation. The main verb is in the base form with both regular and irregular verbs.

I walked.	I did not **walk**.
I went.	I did not **go**.

The contraction of **did not** is **didn't**.

Language in Transition

Nowadays, it is common to use contractions for both spoken and informal written English. Use the full form for formal written English or for emphasis.

a school bag   a coat   math   to meet   to tell   to eat

A. Match the base form and the irregular affirmative form of the past tense.

1.	leave	a)	rode
2.	sit	b)	rang
3.	drive	c)	wore
4.	stand	d)	got off
5.	sing	e)	made
6.	make	f)	saw
7.	wear	g)	drove
8.	speak	h)	left
9.	know	i)	waited
10.	get off	j)	stood
11.	ride	k)	heard
12.	see	l)	knew
13.	hear	m)	sang
14.	ring	n)	spoke
15.	wait	o)	sat

B. Put the sentences in the negative form. Use the contraction.

The bus left early.   The bus **didn't leave** early.

1. The bus driver drove dangerously.
2. The passengers sat at the front of the bus.
3. The driver knew all the passengers.
4. We sang quiet songs during the bus ride.
5. He saw a person running after the bus.
6. The driver spoke to the man behind him.
7. They waited in the rain for half an hour.
8. You rode your bicycle to work every day last year.
9. We heard the siren of a police car.
10. The driver wore a uniform with a hat.
11. She rang the bell three times.
12. The old lady stood for the whole ride.
13. The driver made a mistake and had an accident.
14. We left before the five o'clock rush hour.
15. We got off at the last bus stop.

| to wait for | to ring | to sing | a uniform | a siren | to wear |

C. Some sentences have errors. Find the errors and correct them.

1. She didn't rode her bicycle to work yesterday.
2. They didn't wait for everybody to arrive.
3. Janet didn't wore her coat this morning.
4. He told us that Harry didn't saw the accident.
5. Miguel and Susanna didn't understood English then.
6. They were always late. They didn't tried to come on time.
7. The bus driver didn't hear me ring the bell.
8. Yesterday we didn't wanted to walk to work.
9. Iwan didn't spoke English when he arrived.
10. I didn't know that your name was the same as mine.

UNDERSTAND: Simple Past Tense Question Form

Use the simple past tense to ask questions about events that were completed in past time.

Did you finish all your homework yesterday?

Signal past time by using **did** before the subject of the sentence. Use the base form of the main verb.

You **ate** breakfast early.   **Did** you **eat** breakfast early?

A. Match the base form and the irregular present simple form of the verbs.

1. read	a) drank
2. feel	b) left
3. work	c) watched
4. win	d) had
5. pay	e) woke up
6. take	f) tried
7. spend	g) spent
8. drink	h) said
9. eat	i) ate
10. have	j) won
11. watch	k) read
12. wake up	l) worked
13. say	m) felt
14. try	n) paid
15. leave	o) took

to win   to pay   to drink   to take   to wake up   an accident

B. Read the story about Ben's summer in Paris. Then make questions with the verbs that are in bold type.

Ben Taylor was very lucky. He entered a contest and **won** a trip to Paris. Ben **spent** last summer in Paris. He **loved** his morning routine. He usually woke up early because he **liked** to have time for breakfast. He **went** to a café near his hotel for breakfast. He usually **had** coffee and croissants. Ben always **sat** on the terrace of the cafe. He **ordered** coffee and **read** the newspaper. After he finished his coffee, Ben **paid** the bill and left.

What did Ben win?

1. What ______________________________________?
2. Where ______________________________________?
3. What ______________________________________?
4. Why ______________________________________?
5. Where ______________________________________?
6. What ______________________________________?
7. Where ______________________________________?
8. What ______________________________________?
9. What ______________________________________?
10. When ______________________________________?

C. These sentences have errors. Find the errors and correct them.

1. Where did you went with your friends last night?
2. Why did you left the party so early on Friday?
3. Did you watched that movie on television last night?
4. Did everyone drank that strong coffee?
5. What time did you woke up this morning?
6. Where did she sat in the last class?
7. Did Jennifer spent all her money at the mall?
8. How much did you paid for that ticket?
9. How did they felt after the game yesterday?
10. How much did they won in the lottery last week?

a café

a croissant

a terrace

a mall

a lottery ticket

a party

UNDERSTAND: "Used to" + Verb for Habitual Actions in the Past

Use **used to** + the base form of the main verb to contrast past habits and present activities.

> She **used to visit** Paris every summer when she was a child.

When past habits continue in the present, use **still** + the base form of the present tense of the verb.

> She **still visits** Paris every summer.

Use the negative form of the present tense of the verb **+ anymore** for past habits that do not continue today. Look at the examples.

> She **used to visit** Paris every summer when she was a child.
>
> She **still visits** Europe on holiday when she can.
>
> She **doesn't visit** Europe on holiday **anymore**.

A. Complete a chart of activities. Check (✔) the activities that you used to do in the past. Put another check (✔) for activities you still do. Put an ✘ for activities you don't do anymore.

Activity	I used to do	I still do	I don't do anymore
1. take my lunch to school	✔		
2. watch TV a lot			
3. have a pet			
4. visit my aunt			
5. ride a bicycle			
6. celebrate my birthday			
7. speak another language			
8. travel by bus every day			
9. fight with my sister			
10. feel afraid of snakes			
11. smoke cigarettes			
12. stay up late			
13. go to a lot of parties			
14. play a team sport			
15. do exercise			
16. live in a house			
17. live in the country			
18. take music lessons			
19. walk to school			
20. eat junk food			

a pet   to celebrate   to exercise   the country   junk food   to fight

B. Work in pairs. Talk about the things you used to do. Then write five sentences about things you used to do. Write about whether you do or don't do those things today.

I used to take my lunch to school, but I don't anymore.

C. Write five sentences about your partner.

She used to ride a bicycle to school and she still does.

D. Read the paragraphs. Then answer the questions **T** (true) or **F** (false). Correct information that is false.

Pablo started university last semester. He is enjoying his new experience at school but he is very busy with all his courses. There are a lot of activities he used to do before that he can't do anymore. For example, he used to play soccer every weekend, but now he plays only once a month. He used to meet his friends every day after school. Now he can only see them on the weekend.

Pablo used to be a tennis instructor for children, but he had to stop that activity and pay attention to his studies. Pablo feels that he used to have a lot more free time than he has now. He used to go to movies and concerts a lot more often than he does now. He doesn't go to movies or concerts anymore. Sometimes he misses the fun activities he used to do, but he knows he can't do everything!

1. Pablo used to be a university student.
2. Pablo used to be busier before he started university.
3. Pablo used to play soccer every weekend.
4. Pablo used to meet his friends every day.
5. Pablo still sees his friends every day.
6. Pablo used to be a tennis instructor.
7. Pablo still teaches tennis to children.
8. Pablo feels he still has a lot of free time.
9. Pablo goes to a lot of concerts and movies.
10. Pablo misses all the activities he used to do.

| soccer | tennis | a movie | a concert | to teach | busy |

Listening and Speaking: Using Idioms

A New Country

A. Choose an expression that means the same as the words that are in bold type.

1. I moved to a new country. I really **miss** my old friends.
   a) don't have
   b) want to see
   c) know them well

2. Learning a new language is difficult **at first**, but later it is easier.
   a) all the time
   b) sometimes
   c) in the beginning

3. Do your homework **right away** when you get home. Then you can watch TV.
   a) soon
   b) immediately
   c) later

4. I didn't understand all of the movie, but **at least** I understood part of it.
   a) at the minimum
   b) all together
   c) now

5. I need some exercise. I think I'll **take a walk** outside.
   a) go for a walk
   b) think about a walk
   c) walk quickly

6. I like that TV show. I watch it **all the time**.
   a) sometimes
   b) never
   c) very often

7. It's busy downtown. Everyone is **in a hurry**.
   a) moving slowly
   b) going to work
   c) moving quickly

to miss   to understand   a farmer   a boat   a duck   grain

8. At first I didn't know anyone in the class, but I met some people and **made some new friends**.
   a) was happy
   b) met some new people
   c) remembered old friends

9. We really enjoyed ourselves at the party. Everyone **had fun**.
   a) gave a party
   b) had a good time
   c) was tired

B. Listen and answer the questions.
   1. What did Li do when she first came to her new country?
   2. What did she used to do in her country?
   3. What does she miss the most?
   4. Where did she make new friends?

Turn to page 47 for Exercise C.

Ten-Minute Grammar Games

Solve the Problem

Focus: Review past tense verbs.

Students read the paragraph, and then work in pairs to solve the problem.

A farmer wanted to go to market with some ducks and a large bag of grain that he planned to sell. He had a large brown dog with him. He came to a wide river. The only way to cross the river was in a small boat. The boat was so small that the farmer could take only one thing at a time in the boat. He wasn't sure what to do because the ducks were hungry and wanted to eat the grain. The dog was also hungry and wanted to eat the ducks. The farmer solved the problem. How did he get everything across the river?

Is It True?

Focus: Practise verbs with **used to**.

This activity can be done with the whole class or in groups.

Each student writes down three unusual activities. The students write one thing that they really used to do and two things that are false.

Students work in groups. A student reads his or her list aloud. Other students try to guess which activity is true by asking questions. The student answering the questions should try to make it as difficult as possible for the others to guess.

Times Have Changed

Focus: Practise using **used to** for past time.

Students work in groups to make lists in the categories below.

They think of things they used to do as they grew up, and how these things have now changed. Groups can read their ideas to the class.

> At home
> At school
> Outside
> Sports and recreation
>
> At home: We used to play records. Now we play tapes and CDs.
>
> At school: I used to write compositions by hand. Now I write compositions on a computer.

A Great Day

Focus: Review past tense verbs.

Students think of a great day in their lives. They write a paragraph describing in detail what they did, and why the day was great.

They work in small groups to read their paragraph out loud. Other students can ask questions about the great day.

Test Yourself

Simple Past Tense

A. Complete the chart of present tense and past tense affirmative forms of these irregular verbs.

begin	began
become	became
break	broke
_____	brought
buy	bought
catch	_____
choose	chose
come	_____
_____	drank
drive	_____
_____	ate
feel	felt
find	_____
forget	forgot
fly	flew
_____	got

give	gave
go	_____
have	had
hear	_____
know	knew
leave	left
_____	made
meet	met
pay	paid
put	_____
read	read (/ri:d/)
ride	rode
ring	_____
_____	ran
see	saw
sing	sang
_____	sat
speak	spoke
stand	_____
steal	stole
swim	swam
take	_____
teach	taught
tell	told
think	thought
_____	threw
understand	understood
wake	_____
wear	wore
_____	won
write	wrote

B. Complete the conversation. Use the correct form of the verb.

Carla: I really enjoyed that holiday. The guide _____ (tell) us such interesting stories.

Roberto: He didn't _____ (tell) interesting stories. He _____ (tell) boring stories.

Carla: Well anyway, the weather was great. We _____ (swim) in the ocean and _____ (walk) on the beach every day.

Roberto: We didn't _____ (swim) in the ocean and _____ (walk) on the beach every day. We _____ (swim) in the ocean twice, and we walked on the beach once.

Carla: Yes, well… We were lucky. We _____ (have) a fabulous hotel room with a magnificent view of the mountains.

Roberto: We didn't _____ (have) a fabulous hotel room. We _____ (have) a small, hot, stuffy hotel room. And we didn't even _____ (see) the mountains. We _____ (see) a few hills.

Carla: Well, the entertainment was really good. The woman who _____ (sing) opera was excellent, and the people who _____ (dance) ballet were very good too.

Roberto: Actually, the entertainment wasn't that good. The singer was okay, but she didn't _____ (sing) that well. By the way, the people didn't _____ (dance) ballet, they danced jazz.

Carla: Well, we ate some delicious food. The chef _____ (prepare) some wonderful new dishes.

Roberto: The chef didn't _____ (prepare) new dishes. He _____ (prepare) some very spicy dishes.

Carla: Oh, I give up. You tell the story, Roberto!

C. These sentences have errors. Find the errors and correct them.

1. They didn't sent many postcards from their trip.
2. Max and Fred wrotes a lot of letters home.
3. The kids brang their bathing suits with them.
4. Those people didn't spoke English very well.
5. Hiroshi is angry because someone stealed his camera.
6. He didn't wants to make a report to the police.
7. I didn't saw the ocean during my last trip.
8. Nobody understand when I spoke Japanese.
9. Their vacation ended very suddenly when they lose their money.
10. The guide didn't told us the history of that monument.

"Used to"

Fill in the blanks with **still** + the present tense or **used to** + the base form of the verb.

1. We _____ (go) to the movies every weekend, but now it is too expensive.
2. She always wore her hair long when she was young and she _____ (wear) it long now.
3. Mr. Richards _____ (live) in New York, but now he lives in Florida.
4. I _____ (find) his stories interesting, but I find them less exciting nowadays.
5. When Laura was living in Japan, she _____ (practise) Japanese every day.
6. Pierre knows that smoking cigarettes is bad for his health, but he _____ (smoke) twenty cigarettes a day.
7. We _____ (enjoy) going on vacation with our parents, but we prefer to go alone now.
8. Some things we _____ (do) as children make us laugh today.

9. Most people remember games that they _____ (play) when they were children.
10. I used to speak French every day when I lived in Paris and I _____ (speak) French regularly in Montreal.

Idioms

Complete the paragraph by using idioms. Use the correct form of these expressions to help you.

to miss someone	at first	right away
at least	to take a walk	all the time
to be in a hurry	to make friends	to have fun

Last month, my sister Maria moved to another city to study English. At _____ I really _____ her a lot. Of course I still think about her, but at _____ I don't think about her all _____ now.

When she arrived, she wrote me a letter _____ to say that she _____ me, but that she had a chance to _____ in her English class. She said that she and her new friends _____ together on the weekends. Sometimes she goes to the movies or _____ with her friends. She is lucky to live in a small town because people are not usually in _____.

Score for Test Yourself: _____
50

Note: Answers in Sections A and B of Simple Past Tense are worth half a point each.

[○ ○] # Listening and Speaking: Using Idioms

A New Country

C. Listen and write the missing words.

Maria: How do you feel here, Li? Do you _____ your country?
Li: Well, I did at _____, Maria. I took a language course right _____, so I learned to speak English. At _____ I can communicate.
Maria: Do you miss the things you used to do in your country?
Li: Yes. I used to _____ long walks all the _____. Here, everyone is in a _____. I never go for a walk.
Maria: What do you miss the most?
Li: I _____ my old friends.
Maria: Well, you met some nice people in your English class.
Li: Yes. I _____ some new friends, and we have a lot of _____ together.

D. Practise the conversation with a partner.

E. Work with a partner. Write a conversation about living in a new place. Use as many expressions as you can.

4

Comparison of Adjectives
Question Word "Which"
Pronouns "One" and "Ones"

Adjective	Comparative form	Superlative form
Short adjectives	-er	the -est
tall	tall**er**	the tall**est**
fast	fast**er**	the fast**est**
smart	smart**er**	the smart**est**
strong	strong**er**	the strong**est**
Long adjectives	+ more – less	the most the least
difficult	**more** difficult **less** difficult	**the most** difficult **the least** difficult
interesting	**more** interesting **less** interesting	**the most** interesting **the least** interesting
attractive	**more** attractive **less** attractive	**the most** attractive **the least** attractive
Irregular		
good	better	the best
bad	worse	the worst
far	farther	the farthest
little	less	the least

Word Power

A. Work with a partner. Name the sports.

B. Use these adjectives to describe the sports in the picture. You can use more than one adjective for each.

dangerous	slow	fast
difficult	boring	challenging
exciting	violent	dirty
graceful	tiring	satisfying

Understanding Grammar

UNDERSTAND: **Comparative Form of Adjectives**

Adjective	Comparative form	Superlative form
Short adjectives	-er	the -est
tall	tall**er**	the tall**est**
fast	fast**er**	the fast**est**
smart	smart**er**	the smart**est**
strong	strong**er**	the strong**est**
Long adjectives	+ more – less	the most the least
difficult	**more** difficult **less** difficult	**the most** difficult **the least** difficult
interesting	**more** interesting **less** interesting	**the most** interesting **the least** interesting
attractive	**more** attractive **less** attractive	**the most** attractive **the least** attractive
Irregular		
good	better	the best
bad	worse	the worst
far	farther	the farthest
little	less	the least

dangerous	difficult	graceful	violent	tiring	dirty

Use the comparative forms of adjectives to compare two people or things that are unequal. There are two ways to make comparative adjectives.

Add **er** to short adjectives (one or two syllables) to form the comparative. Use **than** after the adjective in a comparative sentence.

Bijan is strong**er than** Ali.

Use **more** or **less** before adjectives with more than two syllables.

Use **than** after the adjective in a comparative sentence.

Weight-lifting is **more** difficult **than** running.

> **TEACHER'S BOX:** Some adjectives can form the comparative and superlative forms as either short or long adjectives: **tastier** or **more tasty**. Rules for irregular spelling of comparative forms appear in Appendix 1, page 210.

A. Write the correct form of the adjective.

1. Frank is 25. Bob is 18. Frank is _____ (old) than Bob.
2. Gardening is _____ (satisfying) than cleaning the garage.
3. Tennis is _____ (hard) than badminton.
4. Swimming is _____ (dangerous) than ski jumping.
5. Wrestlers are _____ (fat) than high jumpers.
6. Bread is _____ (tasty) than ice cream.
7. A hundred-dollar bill is _____ (unusual) than a thousand-dollar bill.
8. Watching TV is _____ (enjoyable) than washing the dishes.
9. The water in a swimming pool is _____ (warm) than the water in a lake.
10. A computer is _____ (efficient) than a typewriter.

B. Write sentences comparing the sports with the adjective given.

alpine skiing/cross-country skiing (slow)

Cross-country skiing is slower than alpine skiing.

1. walking/running (exhausting)
2. running in a race/running alone (challenging)
3. figure skaters/boxers (violent)
4. basketball players/runners (tall)
5. football players/divers (graceful)

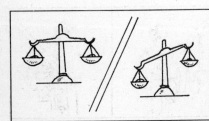   

equal   unequal   badminton   wrestling   a swimming pool   a lake

6. baseball/soccer (slow)
7. sprinters/distance runners (fast)
8. skiing/jogging (expensive)
9. golf/tennis (exciting)
10. hockey/baseball (rough)

UNDERSTAND: **Comparisons with "As" + Adjective + "As"**

Use the form **as** + base form of adjective + **as** to compare two things that are equal.

   Maria is **as** strong **as** Junko.

Use the form **not as** + base form of adjective + **as** to compare unequal things in the negative.

   Yumi is**n't as** old **as** Joseph.

Complete these sentences. Choose **as** + adjective + **as** for things that are equal or **not as** + adjective + **as** for things that are not equal.

1. Walking upstairs is _____ walking downstairs. (easy)
2. Travel by bus is _____ travel by subway. (expensive)
3. Carla and Mia are twins. Carla is _____ Mia. (tall)
4. A bicycle is _____ a car. (fast)
5. Doing homework is _____ going to a party. (interesting)
6. Tennis is _____ hockey. (rough)
7. A diver is _____ a gymnast. (graceful)
8. Eating in a restaurant is _____ eating at home. (cheap)
9. An amateur athlete is _____ a professional athlete. (rich)
10. Football is _____ hockey. (violent)

Language in Transition

When pronouns are used in comparisons, the choice of pronoun is more flexible today than it was in the past. Either the subject or the object pronoun is considered correct in contemporary English: John is taller than **I** (am). John is taller than **me**.

to dive   to ski   to jog   to play golf   upstairs   downstairs

UNDERSTAND: **Superlative Form of Adjectives**

Use the superlative form to compare more than two things to each other.

Add **est** to short adjectives (one or two syllables) to form the superlative. Put **the** before the adjective.

Amal is **the** fast**est** runner.

Use **the most** before adjectives with more than two syllables. Put **the** before **most** in superlative sentences.

Gymnastics is **the most** exciting sport.

A. Write the correct form of the superlative.

1. Nadia was _____ (young) athlete.
2. The Kenyan runner was _____ (less) tired.
3. Mike was _____ (fast) swimmer on the team.
4. The coach was _____ (happy) person there.
5. Katrina was _____ (graceful) skater.
6. Max was _____ (strong) person on his team.
7. Molly is _____ (tall) player on the team.
8. Franco was _____ (skillful) sailor on the boat.
9. Lynda was _____ (talented) golfer in the competition.
10. The Norwegian man was _____ (courageous) participant.

B. Match the description with the sport.

1. basketball   a) the most accurate player wins
2. marathon running   b) the team with the tallest players wins
3. archery   c) the strongest person wins
4. football   d) the best riders win
5. dogsled racing   e) the team with the most goals wins
6. polo   f) the team with the most touchdowns wins
7. weightlifting   g) the runner with the most stamina wins
8. soccer   h) the coldest sport
9. hockey   i) the world's most popular sport

    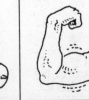

gymnastics   polo   archery   dogsled   weightlifting   strong

UNDERSTAND: **Question Word "Which"**

"Which"

Use **which** + noun to ask questions that give a choice between two or more people or things. The choice can refer to a singular noun or a plural noun.

Which jacket is yours?   the blue jacket

Which gloves are yours?   the red gloves

"Which One"

Use **which one** to ask questions when the person or thing does not need to be named—that is, when gestures can be used or when everyone already knows what you are talking about.

Which one do you want to buy?   the blue one

A. Write the questions about things you **usually** do.

seat/you have   Which seat do you have?

1. game/you watch
2. team/he prefers
3. foods/they eat
4. friends/you invite
5. day/she goes

6. sport/Jim likes best
7. pool/Sharon goes to
8. team/he plays for
9. player/he likes best
10. league/Helen competes in

B. Some sentences have errors. Find the errors and correct them.

✗ Which sports you practise?   Which sports do you practise?

1. Which day does you play soccer?
2. Which coach do he to study with?
3. Which game do they play?
4. Which players do they cheer?
5. Which county she represents?

6. Which tennis racket do he use?
7. Which helmet does he have?
8. Which team does he play for?
9. Which skates you like?
10. Which season you does play in?

a coach   a helmet   skates   gloves   a seat   to cheer

UNDERSTAND: **Pronouns "One" and "Ones"**

Use **one** and **ones** as pronouns to replace the noun with descriptive adjectives. **One** replaces a singular noun. **Ones** replaces a plural noun.

Which **jacket** did you buy?   the blue **one**

Which **skates** did you buy?   the expensive **ones**

> **TEACHER'S BOX:** It is incorrect in English to respond with an adjective alone. **One** or **ones** fills the need for a noun to accompany the adjective:
>
> Which **player** did you meet?   ✗ the tall   ✔ the tall one

Look at the picture of the swim team. Use the clues to identify the people.

the one on the left: **h**

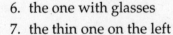

1. the tall one in the back row
2. the blond one with long hair
3. the one in the middle
4. the short ones on the right
5. the fat one

6. the one with glasses
7. the thin one on the left
8. the ones with the towels
9. the short one in the front
10. the muscular one on the left

expensive   cheap   tall   short   glasses   a towel

Listening and Speaking: Using Idioms

What's On?

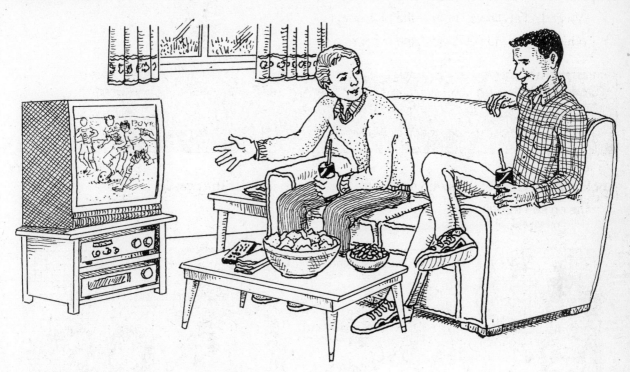

A. Study the expressions used in the sentences.

1. Let's **turn on** the TV. There is a show I want to watch.
2. If you aren't listening to the radio, **turn** it **off**.
3. I want to watch TV tonight. **What's on**?
4. Let's listen to music **for a while**. Later, we can watch TV.
5. If you don't like this show, we can **switch over** to another channel.
6. I'm **tired of** eating at this restaurant. Let's try another one tomorrow.
7. I don't like this restaurant. I **would rather** eat at the restaurant across the street.
8. I don't want to eat in that restaurant. I **can't stand** the food!
9. I like this shirt, and I also like the other one. I can't **make up my mind** which one to buy.
10. Ali: Do you like this shirt?
    Bob: I'm not sure. **I guess so.**

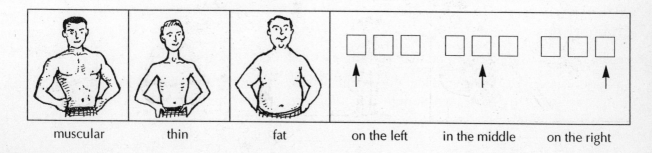

muscular   thin   fat   on the left   in the middle   on the right

58

B. Match the expression to the meaning.

1. to turn on
2. to be tired of
3. what's on?
4. for a while
5. to switch over to
6. to turn off
7. would rather
8. can't stand
9. to make up one's mind
10. guess so/guess not

a) temporarily
b) dislike, hate
c) believe it is true/believe it is false
d) to start equipment
e) prefer
f) to decide
g) to stop equipment
h) to change to
i) to be bored with
j) what's playing?

C. Listen and answer the questions.

1. What does Bob suggest?
2. What is on Channel 13?
3. Why does Bob not want to watch Channel 13?
4. What is Bob tired of watching?
5. What game does Bob dislike?
6. What does Bob suggest they do in the end?

Turn to page 62 for Exercise D.

Ten-Minute Grammar Games

Adjective Options

Focus: Practise using the comparative and superlative forms of adjectives.

Everyone takes three small pieces of paper, and writes one comparative adjective on each:

tallest, most interesting, strongest

The teacher collects the papers and mixes them together.

Students work in pairs. The teacher gives each pair three adjectives. Partners work together to write a short story using the adjectives. The stories should be as imaginative as possible.

Students can read their stories to the class or to a small group.

New York is the most interesting city I have ever visited. It has the tallest buildings, and the most interesting museums and shops. It also has the strongest odours when the garbage isn't picked up!

Comparisons

Focus: Practise using the comparative and superlative form of adjectives.

Students work in pairs. They look at the picture on page 59 and write sentences to compare the things they see. They have a ten-minute time limit. The group with the most imaginative comparisons wins.

An umbrella is more useful in the rain than a tea kettle.

A cat is as big as a chicken.

an apple   **a ball**   **a candle**   **a chicken**

a shovel   **an umbrella**   **a cat**   **an elephant**

a tea kettle   **a broom**   **a bicycle**   **a flashlight**

a spoon   **a box**   **a suitcase**   **a key**

a baby's bottle   **a clothespin**   **a screwdriver**   **a pencil**

What Is It?

Focus: Practise using the comparative and superlative form of adjectives.

Students work in groups. Each person thinks of an object and writes it on a piece of paper.

Other students in the group try to guess what the object is by asking questions using comparative and superlative adjectives:

> It is bigger than a pencil?

> Is it more expensive than a sandwich?

The student being questioned answers only with "yes" or "no." The first student to guess the object wins.

I Spy

Focus: Practise the question word **which** and the pronouns **one** and **ones**.

The teacher begins by picking an object in the class. There should be more than one of this kind of object. For example: "I spy a red chair." Students try to guess which one by asking questions such as, "Is it the one near the door? Is it the one behind your desk?"

The student who gets the right answer gets to choose the next object. Other students take turns guessing which one.

This game can also be played in groups of four or five.

Test Yourself

Comparison of Adjectives

A. These sentences have errors. Find the errors in the comparative forms and correct them.

1. The more famous soccer player of all time is probably Pelé.
2. The Olympic Stadium in Barcelona is more new than the Olympic Stadium in Montreal.
3. The Olympics were once held in Mexico City, which is the most large city in the world.
4. What is a healthiest snack food, chocolate ice cream or fresh fruit?
5. Is it more better to live downtown in a big city or in the suburbs?
6. John is the more moodiest tennis player I know.
7. The less interesting sport of all is curling.
8. One of the more popular sports in the world is football.
9. The sumo wrestlers of Japan are the most fattest athletes.
10. Swimming is the better form of exercise you can get in the summer.

B. Choose the correct spelling of the comparative and superlative forms.

1. prettier/prettyer
2. worste/worst
3. easiest/easyest
4. biger/bigger
5. farer/farther

6. luckyest/luckiest
7. slimer/slimmer
8. dirtyer/dirtier
9. wider/widder
10. youngest/youngiest

C. Paul is trying to choose a health club for his evening and weekend exercise programs. Look at the chart and answer the questions.

Club	Membership	Annual fees	Founded	Location
Muscles Plus	500	$600	1982	5-minute walk
YMCA	1000	$300	1844	10-minute drive
Joe's Gym	300	$400	1926	in the building

1. Which club has the highest fees?
2. Which is farther, Muscles Plus or the YMCA?
3. Which club has the most members?
4. Which club is closest to Paul's apartment?
5. Which club is the least expensive to join?
6. Which club is the newest?
7. Which club is older, Joe's Gym or Muscles Plus?
8. Which club is cheaper, Muscles Plus or Joe's Gym?
9. Which club has the smallest membership?
10. Which club has the most interesting name?

"One" and "Ones"

Some of the sentences have errors in the pronoun forms. Find the errors and correct them.

1. Bob's tennis racket is the ones on the left.
2. The sumo wrestlers are the fat one.
3. Our children are the one with the red towels.
4. The team captain is the short ones on the left.
5. Which one does he cheer for?
6. The player wants to wear that one.
7. Which ones is exercising on the mats?
8. Why don't you try the ones over there?
9. My team is the ones in the blue uniforms.
10. Which ones is in the locker room at the moment?

Idioms

Replace the words in bold type with the correct form of one of these expressions:

to turn on	to switch over to	to make up one's mind
to be tired of	to turn off	guess so/guess not
what's on	would rather	
for a while	can't stand	

1. We can go to an Italian restaurant tonight, but I **would prefer** to go to a Chinese restaurant.
2. Let's look at the newspaper to see **what is playing** tonight.
3. We can watch the movie, but if it's not interesting, we can **change to** the ball game.
4. I like both the shows. I can't **decide** which one to watch.
5. I didn't like that movie on TV yesterday. In fact, I **hate** movies with a lot of violence.
6. Do I want to watch the comedy tonight? **I think so**. I'm not sure.
7. Why don't you **switch on** the TV to see what's on. If there are no good shows tonight, we can **switch it off**.
8. Let's watch the ball game **for now**. Later we can watch the movie.
9. I'm **bored with** Italian food. Let's have Greek food tonight.

Score for Test Yourself: _____
50

Listening and Speaking: Using Idioms

What's On?

D. Listen and write the missing words.

Ali: What do you want to do tonight, Bob? Do you want to watch TV?

Bob: I'm not sure, Ali. Let's turn _____ the TV and see what's _____.

Ali: Hey, there's a tennis match on Channel 13. Let's watch for a _____.

Bob: Nah, it's boring. Let's _____ over to Channel 16 and see if there's a game on.

Ali: Okay. I think the baseball game is on Channel 16.

Bob: I'm tired _____ watching baseball.

Ali: Would you _____ watch the soccer game?

Bob: No, I can't _____ soccer.

Ali: Do you want to watch TV, or not? Make up your _____.

Bob: I guess _____. Let's turn _____ the TV and listen to music on the radio.

E. Practise the conversation with a partner.

F. Write a conversation about watching TV. Use as many expressions as you can.

5

Review Unit

Old Friends

Work in pairs. Choose the appropriate verb and put it in the correct tense. Then practise the dialogue with your partner.

graduate enjoy see think learn try have do take like

Lisa: Hi, Marco. What are you doing here? I _____ you didn't like parties.

Marco: Hi, Lisa. How are you doing? You _____ a good memory. I didn't used to like parties, but I _____ this one.

Lisa: What are you _____ these days? Are you still studying psychology?

Marco: No, I _____ last June. Now I'm working as a school counsellor. What are you up to these days?

Lisa: I'm still _____ to finish my degree. I _____ my last three courses this semester. Tell me about your job. It sounds interesting.

Marco: I _____ it a lot because I _____ a lot of new things every day.

Lisa: What kind of things do you do?

Marco: I meet students to advise them about courses or help them with personal problems. I really like working with young people.

Lisa: Well, it's nice to _____ you again. Good luck with your new job.

The Bus Strike

Choose the correct word for each space.

Last year there was _____ (the, a, some) bus strike in Winnipeg. The first day of _____ (some, a, the) bus strike was the _____ (colder, most cold, coldest) day of the year. The second day we had the _____ (last, worst, better) snow storm of the century. _____ (The, Its, A) snow storm caused _____ (the, a, some) power failure and some parts of the city had no electricity or heating for three days. _____ (The, A, No) people who normally _____ (pushed, rode, waited) the bus had to find other ways to get to their jobs. _____ (A, Some, The) people used car pools and others _____ (bought, took, left) taxis. _____ (The, Not, A) lucky ones stayed home and waited for _____ (a, the, no) storm to end. This was really a strike to remember!

Who Is Doing What?

A. Look at the picture. Make a list of things people are doing.

A tall man with a moustache is waiting for the bus.

B. Work in pairs. Take turns asking questions about what you have described. Then answer the questions.

What is the police officer doing? She is stopping traffic.

World Records Quiz

A. Work in pairs to answer the questions in the quiz.

1. Which rock stars sold the most records and tapes?
   a) The Beatles
   b) The Rolling Stones
   c) Elvis Presley

2. Who were the first humans to fly?
   a) Orville and Wilbur Wright
   b) The Montgolfier Brothers
   c) Charles Lindbergh

3. Which mountain is the highest in the world?
   a) K2 in the Himalayas
   b) Mount McKinley
   c) Mount Everest

4. Which person invented the most objects during his lifetime?
   a) Thomas Edison
   b) Alexander Graham Bell
   c) Leonardo da Vinci

5. Which is the most popular soft drink in the world?
   a) 7-Up
   b) Coke
   c) Pepsi

6. Which artist painted the most pictures?
   a) Pablo Picasso
   b) Rembrandt
   c) Vincent Van Gogh

7. Which activity uses up the most water?
   a) drinking
   b) washing
   c) industry

8. What is the largest organ in the human body?
   a) the heart
   b) the lungs
   c) the skin

B. Read the paragraphs on pages 67-68 to check your answers.

66

Irregular Past Tense Verbs

A. First try the crossword puzzle with the clues given below.

B. If you need help, check the list of irregular past tense verbs at the beginning of Unit 3.

Across

1. The glass fell on the floor and _____.
3. An animal _____ a hole under our house.
5. It was raining hard and everyone _____ wet.
6. A lot of people _____ to the party last Friday.
7. Max knew the way so he _____ the car.
8. Last week I _____ letters to all my friends at home.
10. We were impressed because the guide _____ four languages.
12. Bob cooked a chicken and Karen _____ some dessert.
13. Last year I usually _____ the bus to work.
14. Susan _____ her bag on the table near the door.
15. The school _____ me a registration form by mail.
16. We _____ a lot of work in English last term.
19. When the concert ended, we _____ and applauded loudly.
20. Everyone jumped when the telephone _____.
22. Let's go to a movie. We _____ to a concert last weekend.
23. The guide _____ us not to drink the water.

Down

1. Joe _____ angry when he heard the news.
2. I was surprised that the stranger _____ my name.
4. The teacher was happy that we _____ English well.
5. I forgot my lunch but Sue _____ me a sandwich.
9. It was a nice day so Mike _____ his bicycle to work.
11. Carolina always _____ a dictionary handy in class.
12. I wasn't sure that I knew what he _____.
13. When we finished it was later than we _____.
15. Jack took a piece of bread and _____ butter on it.
17. Yumi is an artist so she _____ a picture on the card.
18. We forgot our coats and soon we _____ cold.
21. We watched the news on TV before we _____ dinner.

World Records Quiz: Answers for Page 65

1. Elvis Presley was the most popular American singer in the history of rock and roll. The Rolling Stones are famous around the world and they are the longest-lasting of the famous groups. But the most famous group ever was the Beatles, who sold over a billion tapes and records. Two of the group members, John Lennon and Paul McCartney, wrote more hit singles than anyone else.

2. Orville and Wilbur Wright were the first people to fly an airplane. Charles Lindbergh was the first person to fly solo across the Atlantic Ocean. But the first people to fly were the Montgolfier brothers from France. They flew in a hot-air balloon in 1783. Actually, they were not the first living beings to travel by air. To test their balloon, the Montgolfier brothers sent a chicken, a duck, and a sheep up in it. Happily, the animals survived the trip and landed safely.

3. At 8610 metres, K2 in Kashmir, is the second highest mountain in the world. Mount McKinley, in Alaska, is lower. It stands 6195 metres high. The world's highest mountain, and the most challenging to climb, is Mount Everest, in Nepal. It stands 8850 metres high. The first people to climb Mount Everest were Edmund Hillary and Tensing Norquay, who reached the top in 1952.

4. Leonardo da Vinci was a genius who lived in the 15th century. This Italian artist drew plans for many things, including a car, an aircraft, and a helicopter, long before they were invented. Alexander Graham Bell also invented many things, including his most famous invention, the telephone. But Thomas Edison was the busiest inventor ever. By the time he died in 1931, he had invented more than 1300 objects, including the electric light bulb.

5. 7-Up and Pepsi are very popular drinks that sell world-wide. Coca-Cola is the world's most popular drink, with sales averaging over 471 billion drinks per day. This represents about 45 percent of the world's market for soft drinks.

6. Vincent Van Gogh, a Dutch painter, was one of the most famous in modern art. Rembrandt was the Netherland's greatest artist. He produced over 1400 drawings and 600 paintings. The Spanish artist Picasso completed the most paintings of all. In his lifetime, he did over 13 000 paintings. This came to about 12 paintings for each month of his life!

7. People need water to survive. A lot of water is consumed by people all over the earth every day. A great deal of water is also used for washing and cleaning things. Surprisingly, however, more water is used by industry than for anything else. For example, it takes 300 litres, or 80 gallons, of water to make the paper for one Sunday newspaper!

8. The heart is a wonderful pump that beats 100 000 times a day sending blood through the body. The lungs provide the body with oxygen. We could not survive without these two organs. The largest organ in the body, however, is the skin. The skin of one regular sized person is so big it covers the equivalent of a surface of 1.9 square metres.

6

Modal Auxiliaries

"Should" and "Must" to Give Advice

"Have to" to Express Necessity

"Don't have to" and "Mustn't" for Lack of Necessity
and for Prohibition

"Can," "Could," "May" to Request Permission

"Would," "Could," "Can" to Make Polite Requests

Modal Auxiliaries "Should" and "Must"

Affirmative		Negative		Negative Contraction	
I should		I should not		I shouldn't	
you should		you should not		you shouldn't	
he should		he should not		he shouldn't	
she should	go	she should not	go	she shouldn't	go
it should		it should not		it shouldn't	
we should		we should not		we shouldn't	
you should		you should not		you shouldn't	
they should		they should not		they shouldn't	

Affirmative		Negative		Negative Contraction	
I must		I must not		I mustn't	
you must		you must not		you mustn't	
he must		he must not		he mustn't	
she must	go	she must not	go	she mustn't	go
it must		it must not		it mustn't	
we must		we must not		we mustn't	
you must		you must not		you mustn't	
they must		they must not		they mustn't	

Semi-modal Auxiliary "Have to"

Affirmative		Negative		Negative Contraction	
I have to		I do not have to		I don't have to	
you have to		you do not have to		you don't have to	
he has to		he does not have to		he doesn't have to	
she has to	go	she does not have to	go	she doesn't have to	go
it has to		it does not have to		it doesn't have to	
we have to		we do not have to		we don't have to	
you have to		you do not have to		you don't have to	
they have to		they do not have to		they don't have to	

Word Power

Work with a partner. Match the words to the picture.

**ambulance   stretcher   doctors   nurses   X-ray   wheelchair
paramedic   cast   crutches   walker   sling   I.V. (intravenous)**

Understanding Grammar

UNDERSTAND: **Modal Auxiliary Verbs**

Modal auxiliary verbs are used to express certain ideas that involve obligation, politeness, possibility, probability, and necessity. Most modals have multiple functions depending on the context of use.

Modals use the base form of the verb. Modals are always put before other verbs in a verb phrase. Only one modal can be used at a time. Some verbs, such as **have to**, are semi-modals and follow different rules.

UNDERSTAND: **Giving Advice Using "Should" and "Must"**

"Should"

Use **should** to give advice or to express opinions. Use the negative form, **should not**, to advise against doing something. The contraction of **should not** is **shouldn't**.

> You **should** see a doctor. (It is my opinion.)
>
> People **shouldn't** smoke. (Doctors advise against it.)

Use modal auxiliaries before the base form of the main verb. The form **should** is used in present or future time.

Present	You **shouldn't close** the window now.
Future	You **should** lock the door when you go out (later).

Affirmative		**Negative**		**Negative Contraction**		**Question**	
I should		I should not		I shouldn't		should I	
you should		you should not		you shouldn't		should you	
he should		he should not		he shouldn't		should he	
she should	go	she should not	go	she shouldn't	go	should she	go?
it should		it should not		it shouldn't		should it	
we should		we should not		we shouldn't		should we	
you should		you should not		you shouldn't		should you	
they should		they should not		they shouldn't		should they	

| crutches | a cast | a sling | a walker | a wheelchair | an IV |

A. Match the problem with the solution.

a toothache   see a dentist

1. a headache
2. feeling tired
3. want to lose weight
4. a broken arm
5. cut finger
6. the 'flu
7. trouble reading
8. a sprained ankle
9. afraid of sunburn
10. feeling thirsty

a) have an X-ray
b) eat less
c) see an eye doctor
d) use crutches
e) take an aspirin
f) have a drink of water
g) sleep in tomorrow
h) get stitches
i) use sunscreen
j) take aspirin, drink juice, stay in bed

B. Write sentences giving advice for these problems. Use **should** or **shouldn't**.

1. Suddenly I'm feeling extremely hungry.   **You should eat.**
2. The weather man says it will be very cold outside tomorrow.
3. Doctors say that smoking is very dangerous to our health.
4. I don't really like hot days very much. I prefer cold weather.
5. It will cost a lot of money to take a taxi downtown.
6. Someone told me that that movie is really boring.
7. I'm exhausted from cross-country skiing all afternoon.
8. Reading in poor light can harm your eyes.
9. I really like to ski in the Rockies more than in the Adirondacks.
10. I love going to resorts where you can sit around the fire.

"Must"

Use **must** to give strong or urgent advice or opinions. Use the negative form, **must not**, to strongly advise against doing something. The contraction of **must not** is **mustn't**. (Don't pronounce the first **t** in **mustn't**.)

You **must** wear a warm coat in winter. (or you will freeze)

You **mustn't** drink that. (It's poison.)

Use modal auxiliaries before the base form of the main verb. The auxiliary verb **must** is used for present or future time.

Present   You mustn't cross the street without looking.

Future   You must be careful when you come to the corner.

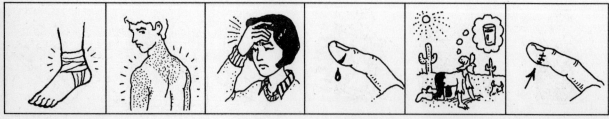

a sprained ankle   sunburn   a headache   a cut   thirsty   stitches

Affirmative	Negative	Negative Contraction
I must you must he must she must it must go we must you must they must	I must not you must not he must not she must not it must not go we must not you must not they must not	I mustn't you mustn't he mustn't she mustn't it mustn't go we mustn't you mustn't they mustn't

A. Look at the conversations. Complete the sentences with **must** or **mustn't**.

1. I am going to Australia.
   Oh really. You _____ forget your passport.

2. It is –30 degrees outside.
   You _____ wear a warm hat and coat.

3. I have diabetes.
   You _____ eat sugar.

4. There is a big exam tomorrow.
   We _____ study hard tonight.

5. Your new jacket is too big for you.
   You can return it, but you _____ have a receipt.

6. You see a beautiful scene and you know you will never return to see it again.
   You _____ take a picture so you will remember it.

7. My sister gets sunburned very easily.
   She _____ sit in the sun.

8. I just got a parking ticket.
   You _____ forget to pay it quickly or it will cost more.

9. I have a bad pain in my back.
   You _____ see a doctor immediately.

10. You have an interview for an important job.
    You _____ arrive for the interview late.

 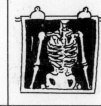   

poison   an X-ray   cross-country ski   a passport   a scene   a receipt

B. Match this advice with the public notices.

1. You must stop here.
2. You mustn't smoke here.
3. You should knock before you enter.
4. You should open the other end.
5. You mustn't park here from 8 o'clock to 10 o'clock.
6. You should be quiet here.
7. You mustn't walk on the grass.
8. You should watch for falling ice.
9. You should be careful of moose.
10. You must show your ticket to the guard.

passengers   to park   between   to knock   danger   a guard

UNDERSTAND: **Obligation Using "Have to"**

Use **have to** to express obligations or actions that are necessary for you to take.

> Mike **has to** be at work at nine o'clock. (It's a company rule.)

> I **have to** go now. (I'm tired.)

Have to is a semi-modal. It does **not** follow the rules for modal formation. Compare the form of **have to** with **must** (a modal). Use **have to** (**has to**) before the base form of the main verb.

Language in Transition

In affirmative statements, the modal **must** is sometimes used to express a stronger form of obligation than **have to: I have to go now or I'll be late. Everyone must be off the streets before the curfew.** Generally, however, the terms are used interchangeably in contemporary English. **Have to** is the common form used to express necessity.

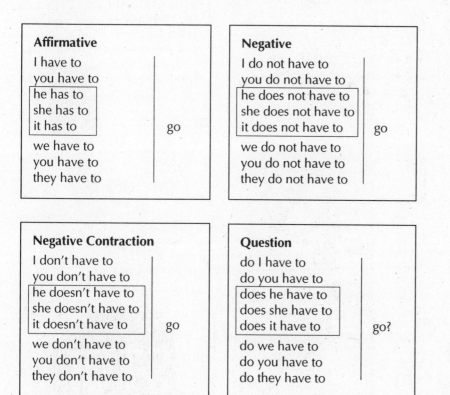

Affirmative

I have to
you have to
he has to
she has to
it has to   go
we have to
you have to
they have to

Negative

I do not have to
you do not have to
he does not have to
she does not have to
it does not have to   go
we do not have to
you do not have to
they do not have to

Negative Contraction

I don't have to
you don't have to
he doesn't have to
she doesn't have to
it doesn't have to   go
we don't have to
you don't have to
they don't have to

Question

do I have to
do you have to
does he have to
does she have to
does it have to   go?
do we have to
do you have to
do they have to

| to smoke | to fall | to be careful | grass | ice | a moose |

A. Andrew is leaving on a trip to Indonesia. Gaby is asking him questions about his arrangements. Match the questions with the answers.

1. What do you have to do before you leave?
2. Why do you have to get a visa to go to Indonesia?
3. What time do you have to be at the airport?
4. Why do you have to be there so early if the plane leaves at 10:00?
5. What time do you have to wake up to get to the airport on time?
6. What do you have to do when you get to the airport?
7. Where do you have to go to check in for your flight?
8. What do you have to do to get your boarding pass?
9. Who do you have to show your boarding pass to?
10. Do you have to change planes during the trip?

a) I have to be there at seven o'clock.
b) Yes, I have to change planes in Chicago and Tokyo.
c) I have to check in with the airline.
d) I have to get a visa.
e) I have to wake up at 5:30 a.m.
f) … because the Indonesian government requires it.
g) I have to show it to the security guard.
h) I have to go to the airline counter.
i) I have to show them my airline ticket.
j) … because it is an international flight.

Language in Transition

Formal written English uses **whom** rather than **who** for the objective case, as in Question 9. In spoken and informal written English, **who** is generally used.

B. Complete the sentences with the correct form of **have to**.

1. Passengers _____ pass through security checks at the airport.
2. All the window seats are taken. That man _____ take an aisle seat.
3. Everyone _____ fasten his or her seat belt during take off.
4. You _____ check in at Gate 97 half an hour before your flight.
5. You _____ stow all hand baggage under the seats before takeoff.
6. Passengers _____ check their baggage before boarding the plane.
7. Mrs. James _____ pay to leave her car in the airport parking garage.
8. International passengers _____ have their customs forms stamped.
9. Passengers _____ wait at the carrousel for their baggage.
10. Rick is vegetarian. He _____ order his meals in advance.

a visa · an airport · to check in · security check · an aisle · to stow

UNDERSTAND: **Prohibition and Lack of Necessity Using "Must not" and "Do not have to"**

"Must not"

Use the negative form **must not (mustn't)** to express prohibitions or strong warnings. The negative form is more commonly used than the affirmative form.

> You **mustn't swim** here. (The water is polluted.)

Use the negative form **must not (mustn't)** to suggest a duty you impose on yourself.

> I **mustn't** forget to thank Mei for her help yesterday.

Put **must not (mustn't)** before the base form of the main verb.

> I **mustn't lose** my temper at the next meeting.

"Do not have to"

Use **don't have to** to say that something is **not necessary**. Follow the rules for forming negatives and questions with the auxiliary verb **do** or **does** and the base form of the main verb.

> I **don't have to** go to work today.

> He **doesn't have to** go to work tomorrow.

A. Choose **mustn't** or **don't have to**.

1. They lock the door at 10:30. We _____ forget our keys.
2. It's a holiday. We _____ go to work today.
3. I had a dentist's appointment today. I _____ go back again until the 16th.
4. You _____ eat that salmon salad. It's not fresh.
5. Anne can walk on her sore leg. She _____ use crutches.
6. The traffic is terrible. You _____ cross the street here.
7. Max does exercise every day. He _____ worry about his weight.
8. Janet has good eyes. She _____ wear glasses to read.
9. If you are French, you _____ have a passport to visit England.
10. This is a no-parking zone. You _____ park your car here.

to fasten   to stamp   to lose one's temper   a carrousel   no-parking zone   keys

B. Some sentences have errors. Find errors in the form of **mustn't** and **don't have to** and correct them.

1. The patient don't have to stay in bed all day.
2. You mustn't to take that medicine between meals.
3. The tourists mustn't stay out in the the sun too long.
4. We don't have to use mosquito repellent very often.
5. I doesn't have to see the doctor this afternoon.
6. Hospital visitors mustn't to make loud noise.
7. Patients with broken bones doesn't always have to wear casts.
8. People don't have wait long for an appointment.
9. You mustn't use the elevator if there is a fire.
10. You doesn't have to wear your coats outside today.

UNDERSTAND: **Using "Can," "Could," and "May" to Request Permission**

Use **can**, **could**, and **may** to make polite requests for permission to do something. **Can** is less formal and is generally used with family and friends.

Put polite requests in question form with the modal (**can**, **could**, or **may**) at the beginning of the sentence. Use the base form of the main verb.

May I use your telephone?

Can we come in now?

Could I borrow your pen?

> **Language in Transition**
>
> Another less common form of polite request is to use the modal **might**. It is rarely used and sounds old fashioned today.

Question Forms for Polite Requests for Permission

Requests for permission using the modal **may** cannot be made with the second person **you** form.

✗ May you come in?

Forms of "May" to Request Permission

may I may he may she may we may they	leave?

a patient   mosquito repellent   a meal   an elevator   quiet   loud

A. Some sentences have errors. Find the errors and correct them.

1. Can he comes with us tomorrow?
2. Could she join the team next year?
3. May you come in now?
4. Can she borrows your umbrella?
5. May I please be excused?
6. Can we leaves the classroom?
7. Could I smoke a cigarette here?
8. May you open the door please?
9. Can we to come in now?
10. Could I join you for lunch?

B. Make polite requests for permission in these situations.

1. You need to use a friend's dictionary.   **May I use your dictionary?**
2. You want to leave the table before other people.
3. You and your friends want permission to leave class early.
4. You want to smoke in a restaurant.
5. You want to use the telephone in a stranger's office.
6. Your sister needs permission to register for classes.
7. Your brother needs to borrow a towel from your friend.
8. You want your friends to stay at your parents' house tonight.
9. You see someone you know in the cafeteria and want to sit down.
10. An old lady needs help with her heavy suitcases.

UNDERSTAND: "Would," "Could," or "Can" for Polite Requests

Use **would**, **could**, or **can** when you want to ask someone to do something for you. The polite request form **would**, **could**, or **can** is often accompanied by the word **please** before the base form of the main verb.

> **Would** you (please) pass me the butter?
>
> **Could** you (please) tell me the time?
>
> **Can you** (please) answer the phone?

It is possible to use **could** or **can** with different pronouns (first, second, third person) to make polite requests. Polite requests with **would** can only be expressed in the second person (**you**).

> ✘ Would she borrow ten dollars?
>
> ✘ Would I borrow ten dollars
>
> ✔ Would you lend me ten dollars?
>
> or   ✔ Could I borrow ten dollars?

An alternative form of polite request is the expression "I wonder if you could ..."

| a cafeteria | a team | a towel | to register | to pass | butter |

Find the sentences with errors and correct them.

1. Could I borrow your dictionary?
2. Would she answer the telephone?
3. Could he waits for us outside?
4. Can you speak more slowly?
5. Would you turn down the television?
6. Could you explain that again?
7. Can you helps me move this desk?
8. Would she give me a receipt?
9. Would you please are careful?
10. Could he tries to arrive on time?

Listening and Speaking: Using Idioms

Under the Weather

A. Find the correct meaning for each idiom.

1. **What's the matter?** You don't look well.
   a) What's the problem?   b) What do you think?

2. In winter many people **catch colds**.
   a) get colds   b) are cold

3. This medicine should help you **feel better** soon. The other medicine made you feel worse.
   a) touch   b) recover

4. The bus is late today. It should be here **by now**.
   a) at this time   b) soon

5. When you are tired or sick, you shouldn't work so hard. You should **take it easy**.
   a) do an easy job   b) relax and rest

6. Julie has a cold. She is **under the weather** today.
   a) feeling cold   b) feeling sick

7. I don't feel well. I may be **coming down with** the 'flu.
   a) getting   b) not getting

8. When you are sick, you should go to the doctor for a **check-up**.
   a) medicine   b) examination

B. Listen and answer the questions.

1. What is wrong with Carla?
2. What does Benito think she should do?
3. What will Carla do if she doesn't feel better?

Turn to page 85 for Exercise C.

| fast | slow | a cold | a check-up | to move | a helmet |

Ten-Minute Grammar Games

Looking for a Roommate

Focus: Practise modal auxiliaries.

1. Students pretend they are looking for someone to share an apartment. They work in pairs to write a list of ten things that are important to them. They should use a modal auxiliary to begin each sentence. They can use the ideas listed below or any others they can think of.

be clean and neat	be a man
have a pet	be a woman
be able to cook	be a student
have a car	provide furniture
smoke	have parties
be vegetarian	

2. In pairs, students write an ad that can go in a newspaper:

   I am looking for someone to share my apartment. Must be female. Can be a student. Mustn't smoke. Can have a small pet, but mustn't have a large dog. Should be willing to cook and provide kitchen equipment. Shouldn't be a vegetarian. May have parties only on the weekend.

What Is It?

Focus: Use modal auxiliaries.

1. Students work in pairs. They think of a game or sport that they know, and write down as many things about the game as they can, using modal auxiliaries. These can include:

   rules for playing
   safety regulations
   equipment needed
   protocol (what is polite and impolite)

   They write four things about the game or sport on a piece of paper, without writing the name of the game or sport.

   To win, you **have to** score more goals than the other team.
   You **should wear** a helmet.
   You **must never hit** another player.
   You **can play** in teams of seven or more.

2. Students take turns reading the rules of their game out loud to the class. Other students try to guess the name of the game or sport.

Objects and Uses

Focus: Practise modal auxiliaries.

Students look at the list below. Working with a partner, they choose five of the items, and list at least three ways to use each one. They should be as imaginative as they can.

I could use the scotch tape to hold up the hem of my skirt.

scotch tape
a safety pin
soap
a glass of water
a day to yourself
a paper clip
a notebook
a spoon
a lemon
a cellular phone
a cardboard box
an eraser
a friend
a piece of chocolate
a $5.00 bill
two hours

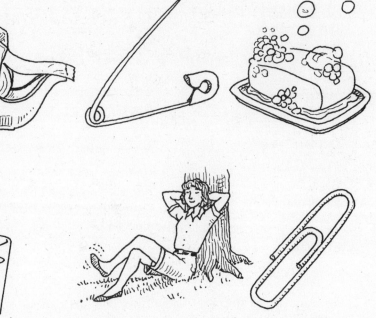

Test Yourself

"Should" to Give Advice

A. Look at the problems below. Give the person advice with **should** and **shouldn't**. Use the ideas on the right to help you.

1. I have an exam next week.   study
2. She has a bad cold.   come to class
3. He has a bad headache.   take an aspirin
4. They are very impatient.   try to relax
5. The water is freezing.   go swimming
6. I want to lose weight.   have dessert
7. It is raining very hard.   take an umbrella
8. We are really hungry.   cook a good dinner
9. My house is dirty.   clean it up
10. They didn't study.   expect to pass

B. Some sentences have errors. Find the errors and correct them.

1. They shouldn't to go outside without coats.
2. She have to do more aerobic exercise.
3. I have to write home at least once a week.
4. Mike has the car so we don't have to walk home.
5. Everyone should to eat a healthy breakfast.
6. We mustn't to stand in the rain without an umbrella.
7. Mike should drives because it is his car.
8. People doesn't have to eat dessert all the time.
9. He shouldn't goes outside without a warm hat.
10. I mustn't forgets to call home before I leave.

Polite Requests

A. Choose the correct sentence.

1. a) Excuse me, could you please tell me the time?
   b) Excuse me, should you please tell me the time?

2. a) Can you show me where to get the bus downtown?
   b) Are you show me where to get the bus downtown?

3. a) Would we leave now or do we have to wait for something?
   b) Could we leave now or do we have to wait for something?

4. a) I can't hear you. May you please speak louder?
   b) I can't hear you. Can you please speak louder?

84

5. a) Can we have a wake-up call for eight o'clock please?
   b) Would we have a wake-up call for eight o'clock please?

6. a) Could you please repeat that question?
   b) Should you please repeat that question?

7. a) May everyone please stop talking immediately?
   b) Would everyone please stop talking immediately?

8. a) Can you please give me your homework next class?
   b) Should you please give me your homework next class?

9. a) May you please come to class on time in future?
   b) Would you please come to class on time in future?

10. a) Could I ask you for some help with this problem?
    b) Would I ask you for some help with this problem?

B. Some sentences have errors. Find the errors and correct them.

1. Would I borrow some money from you?
2. May you please speak up? We can't hear you in the back.
3. Hey John, can I borrow your camera for a few days?
4. Would I see you about that after class?
5. Excuse me, would you please tell me the time, sir?
6. Could I help you carry that heavy package?
7. Can you move that a little more to the left?
8. May we look at the dessert menu now please?
9. Would I please leave my car here while I shop?
10. Could they write their exam next week instead?

Idioms

Use an idiom to replace the words in bold. Use the correct form of the idioms below to help you.

What's the matter?
to catch a cold
to get/feel/be/better, worse
by now
to slow down
to take it easy
to feel under the weather
to come down with something
a check-up

1. We have been driving for a long time. We should be there **by this time**.
2. You are driving too fast. Please **go more slowly**.
3. I have a headache and a sore throat. I'm feeling **sick** today.

4. You look tired today. Why don't you **take a rest** this afternoon.

5. Every year I go to the doctor to have **an examination**.

6. After you took the aspirin, did your headache **become better**?

7. If you have a sore throat, you may **be getting** a cold.

8. A lot of people in the class have the 'flu. I hope I don't **get sick** too.

9. I don't feel well today, but I'm sure I will **be better** tomorrow.

10. **What's the problem?** You don't look happy today.

Score for Test Yourself: _____
50

Listening and Speaking: Using Idioms

Under the Weather

C. Listen and write the missing words.

Benito: What's the matter Carla? You don't look well.

Carla: It's this cold. I _____ it last week. I should _____ better by _____, but instead I feel _____.

Benito: Maybe you're working too hard. You should take _____ easy.

Carla: Yeah, I guess you're right. I really should take it _____ when I'm feeling _____ the weather like this.

Benito: Do you think you're coming _____ with the 'flu? Maybe you should call the doctor.

Carla: Well, if I don't feel _____ tomorrow, I'll make an appointment for a _____.

D. Practise the dialogue with a partner.

E. Write a dialogue about getting sick. Use as many expressions as you can.

 **7** Past Continuous with "When" and "While"
"Another," "Other," "Others"

Past Continuous Aspect

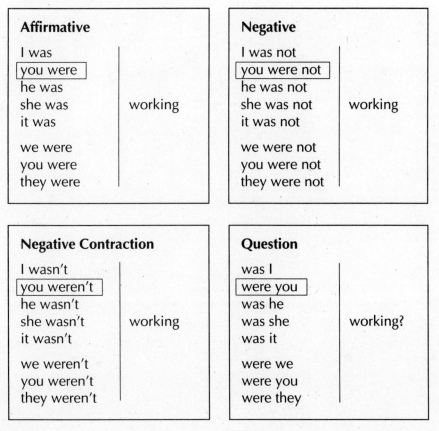

Affirmative

I was
you were
he was
she was
it was

we were
you were
they were

working

Negative

I was not
you were not
he was not
she was not
it was not

we were not
you were not
they were not

working

Negative Contraction

I wasn't
you weren't
he wasn't
she wasn't
it wasn't

we weren't
you weren't
they weren't

working

Question

was I
were you
was he
was she
was it

were we
were you
were they

working?

Word Power

Work with a partner. Describe the problems that you see in the pictures.

Understanding Grammar

UNDERSTAND: **Past Continuous Tense**

Use the past continuous to focus on an action **in progress in the past**. Use the past continuous for an action that was not finished when it was interrupted in the past.

> I was studying until midnight last night.
>
> I was studying when the phone rang.

Use the past form of the auxiliary verb **be** (**was**, **were**) to show past time. Use the ending **ing** to show continuous aspect.

It **was raining** hard yesterday.

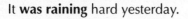

past   continuous

I was	
you were	
he was	
she was	
it was	working
we were	
you were	
they were	

TEACHER'S BOX: See rules for spelling the continuous form in Appendix 1, page 209.

| to study | midnight | a flood | an accident | a snowstorm | rain |

A. Put the verbs in the past continuous form.

1. The neighbours _____ (make) a lot of noise last night.
2. I heard that it _____ (rain) hard all day yesterday.
3. Many people _____ (sleep) on the subway this morning.
4. The tourists _____ (hurry) to get out of the rain.
5. My sister _____ (sit) in the back seat of the car.
6. Everyone _____ (carry) an umbrella this morning.
7. My parents _____ (listen) to their favourite music.
8. I couldn't sleep. You _____ (snore) all night.
9. Jack and I _____ (study) together yesterday afternoon.
10. The radio _____ (work) the last time I tried it.

B. At 10 p.m. last night there was an earthquake. Look at the pictures. Write sentences about what the people were doing at 10 p.m.

| quiet | noisy | a radio | to listen to | to snore | an earthquake |

UNDERSTAND: **Past Continuous Negative**

Use the past continuous negative to say that an action was **not** taking place in the past.

It **was not raining** this morning.

Use the past tense form of the auxiliary verb **be** + **not** for negation. Use the **ing** form of the main verb.

We **were not driving** too fast.

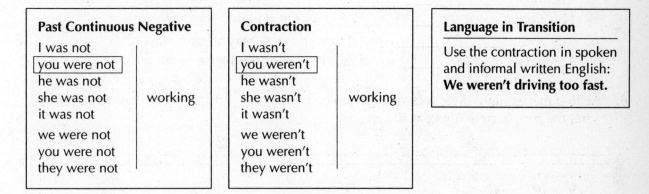

Past Continuous Negative			Contraction			Language in Transition
I was not			I wasn't			Use the contraction in spoken and informal written English: **We weren't driving too fast.**
you were not			you weren't			
he was not			he wasn't			
she was not	working		she wasn't	working		
it was not			it wasn't			
we were not			we weren't			
you were not			you weren't			
they were not			they weren't			

A. Write the sentences in the negative form. Use the contraction.

1. They _____ (try) to sleep in yesterday.
2. He _____ (work) in his father's store last night.
3. Susan _____ (drive) too slowly.
4. You _____ (kick) the back of my chair.
5. We _____ (run) in the park before breakfast.
6. Your friends _____ (walk) too quickly.
7. She _____ (look) for her sunglasses.
8. I _____ (try) to help her find her glasses.
9. They _____ (watch) television all evening.
10. You _____ (shop) all morning.

to kick   a park   to look for   sunglasses   TV   to shop

B. Match the questions and the answers.

1. How did the accident happen?
2. How did you know that the neighbours were away?
3. Why were you surprised to see your sister here?
4. How did you know it was cold out?
5. Why did the store lose money?
6. Why are these pictures so dark?

a) The camera wasn't working very well.
b) People were wearing coats and hats.
c) She said she was spending the day at home.
d) Their newspapers were lying on the doorstep.
e) Nobody was shopping there anymore.
f) The driver wasn't paying attention.

UNDERSTAND: **"When" and "While" with the Past Continuous and Simple Past**

Use the past continuous and the simple past together to show that one action interrupted another action.

> While we were watching the game, it began to rain.
>
> When it began to rain, we were standing at the bus stop.

Use **while** to indicate duration.

Note: Use **during** + a noun phrase.

> during the meal

Use **while** + a verb phrase.

> while I was driving to work

Use **when** to indicate a specific time.

> When the accident happened, my friend was driving.

Language in Transition

When is sometimes substituted for **while** by native speakers.

A. Look at the pictures of Mario's Disastrous Day and match the two parts of the sentences.

1. While he was having a shower,
2. While he was getting out of the shower,
3. When he answered the phone,
4. While he was making the coffee,
5. While he was waiting for the bus,
6. When the bus came,
7. While he was riding in the elevator,
8. When he arrived at work,
9. When he sat down at his desk,
10. While he was sitting on the floor,

a) his boss was looking at his watch.
b) it started to rain.
c) a client came into his office.
d) he slipped on the soap.
e) the toast burned.
f) the phone rang.
g) it was full.
h) it was the wrong number.
i) the chair broke.
j) it got stuck between floors.

| a doorstep | a shower | a boss | a client | to slip | soap |

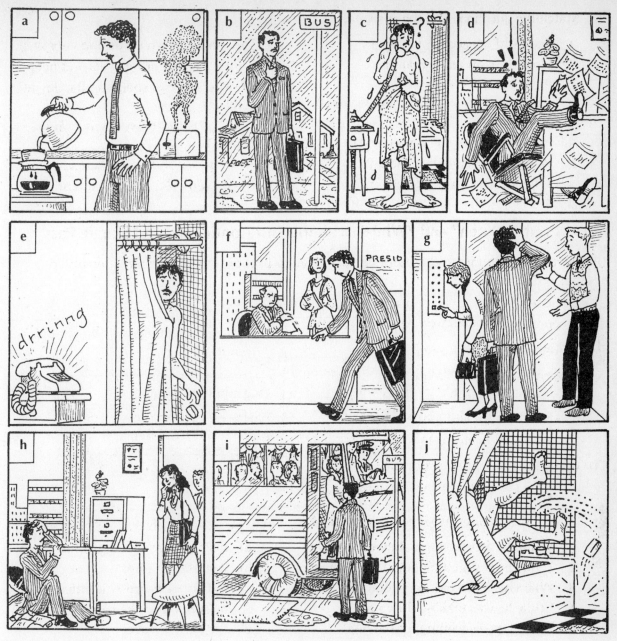

Mario's Disastrous Day

B. Put the pictures in order.

C. Tell your partner the story of Mario's Disastrous Day. Use the pictures to help you.

to burn   full   empty   to break   to be stuck   floors

UNDERSTAND: Adjectives "Another" and "Other" and Pronoun "Others"

Another, other, and **others** are used to suggest an alternative:

The class isn't here. It's in **another** room.

Use **another** as an adjective before a singular noun:

I didn't mean that apple. I meant **another** apple.

Use **other** as an adjective with a plural noun:

Some apples are green. **Other apples** are red.

Use **others** as a pronoun to replace a plural noun:

Some apples are red. **Others** are green.

> **TEACHER'S BOX:** The adjective **another** is also used to mean something additional: That was good. Can I have **another** one?
>
> *Note:* Adjectives are always singular in English, so the adjective form **other** does not have an **s**.

A. Choose the adjective **another** or **other** to complete the sentences.

1. Our neighbours moved last month. _____ family lives there now.
2. The dictionary says that _____ word for "quick" is "rapid."
3. Some people can learn languages quickly. _____ people take longer.
4. I am really tired. I can't study _____ minute.
5. Our car broke down last month. We bought _____ one yesterday.
6. We chose a dictionary. They chose _____ books.
7. If that program isn't on, we can watch _____ channel.
8. I solved the first problem. The _____ problems were too hard.
9. I'm busy right now but we can talk _____ time.
10. We crossed the street quickly. _____ tourists waited for the light to change.

B. Use **another** or **other** as adjectives. Use **others** as a pronoun.

1. It wasn't Air Canada. It was _____ airline.
2. It wasn't that movie. It was _____ one.
3. Some cities are crowded. _____ aren't.
4. _____ students can do the work if John is busy.
5. Some jokes are funny. _____ are not.
6. The athlete is going to run _____ races this year.
7. I can't help you right now. Maybe I can _____ time.
8. If you miss the ten o'clock flight, there is _____ at 10:30.
9. I don't like this store. Let's look in some _____.
10. Some people are friendly. _____ are grouchy.

crowded

an athlete

friendly   grouchy

to choose

a race

C. Some sentences have errors. Find the errors and correct them.

1. The duty free store doesn't have another colours.
2. The others passengers are on standby for the flight.
3. The man lost his passport and had to get the another one.
4. The flight attendant asked if I wanted another drink.
5. Some people like quiet holidays. Other prefer excitement.
6. Other seat is available in the non-smoking section.
7. Are you going on another cruise next year?
8. This map is not very good. Let's get another one.
9. My visa expires soon. I need to get other one.
10. This tour is too expensive. Let's take another one.

Listening and Speaking: Using Idioms

What Happened to You?

A. Find the meaning for each idiom.

1. The show starts at 7:00 **sharp**. Please don't be late.
   a) exactly
   b) approximately
2. I think my alarm clock is broken. It didn't **go off** this morning.
   a) fall off the table
   b) ring
3. I phoned you a few times last night, but I couldn't **get through**.
   a) reach the phone
   b) get a reply
4. I know you didn't mean to cause a problem. It's just **one of those things**.
   a) an accident
   b) a huge problem
5. I have the paper you need. Just **give me a minute** to find it.
   a) give me your watch
   b) give me some time
6. Did you hear what I said? **Never mind**, it wasn't that important.
   a) never forget
   b) don't be concerned
7. It's warm in this room. Why don't you **take off** that heavy sweater?
   a) remove
   b) bring

B. Listen and answer the questions.

1. What time were Tom and Max supposed to meet?
2. Why did Max sleep in?
3. Why couldn't Max get through?
4. What do they have to do today?

Turn to page 101 for Exercise C.

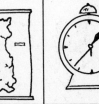

| expensive | cheap | a map | an alarm clock | to put on | to take off |

Ten-Minute Grammar Games

What Were They Wearing?

Focus: Practise past continuous aspect.

Students work in pairs to solve the following puzzle.

Five students were filling out registration forms for courses at night school. Suddenly the fire alarm rang and everyone had to run outside. When the secretary came back she realized that she knew which courses the students wanted to register for, but she didn't know their names. All she remembered was what they were wearing. With the clues below, help the secretary match the students with the courses.

1. Ali Bouanba was wearing a red sweater.
2. Maria De Rosa was signing up for a TOEFL course.
3. The student in Beginners wasn't wearing a yellow sweater.
4. The student with the green sweater was registering for Advanced English.
5. Ray Pinto was not wearing a yellow sweater.
6. Alvaro Trueba was wearing a blue sweater, not a black one.
7. Ray Pinto was registering for Writing Workshop.
8. The student with the blue sweater was registering for Language Lab.

	Ali	Maria	Ray	Alvaro	Junka
Course					
Sweater					

Sentence Ends

Focus: Practise past continuous aspect with **when** and **while**.

Students work in pairs. They take ten minutes to think of ideas to complete the following sentences. They should be as creative as they can. Afterwards, they can read their sentences to a group or to the class as a whole.

1. When I woke up yesterday, I was amazed to see…
2. While I was studying yesterday, I remembered…
3. When I looked at the front page of the newspaper last night, I saw…
4. When the phone rang yesterday, I was surprised to hear from…
5. While I was waiting for the bus yesterday, I noticed…
6. When I arrived in class this morning, I realized…
7. When I opened my schoolbag in class, I found…

8. While I was eating supper yesterday, I…
9. While I was watching TV yesterday, I learned…
10. When the doorbell rang yesterday, I was astonished to see…

Option: Work in groups to write a short story using these or other sentences beginning with **when** and **while**.

What Was Happening?

Focus: Practise past continuous aspect.

Students work individually to study the picture for two minutes, and try to remember what everyone was doing. Then they turn to page 98.

Yesterday the teacher arrived late. All the students thought she wasn't coming that day.

Students write sentences about what everyone was doing before the teacher arrived. They should not look back at page 97 until they have finished.

Test Yourself

Past Continuous

A. Complete the story with the verbs below. Use the past continuous form of the verb.

The Football Game

hold   cheer   run   fly   pass   take   sell   sit   use   jump

You should have been there! It was a huge crowd. People in front _____ up and down. One man had a camera. He _____ pictures. Someone else _____ peanuts. We _____ in the back row. A lady near us _____ binoculars. The teenagers in front of us _____ up a sign.

It was exciting to be there with all that action. Our team _____ all over the field. Player 36, Player 16, and Player 19 _____ the ball. The crowd _____ wildly. Suddenly I looked down and the ball _____ between the goalposts. What a great game!

B. Some sentences have errors. Find the errors and correct them.

1. It weren't raining before the game started.
2. We were having a wonderful time before it rained.
3. The man and the woman was sitting on the bench.
4. My father was speaking on his cellular phone.
5. Two players were running across the field.
6. Max's brother were taking pictures of everyone.
7. Those women wasn't shopping at the mall this morning.
8. My friends was cheering the football players.
9. A lot of people was eating popcorn during time out.
10. The security guards wasn't checking people's identity.

C. Put **when** or **while** in the sentences.

1. I was walking home _____ I saw an accident.
2. _____ I was looking at the accident, the police arrived.
3. _____ they saw an injured man, they called an ambulance.
4. _____ they were waiting for the ambulance, they stopped all the traffic.
5. The ambulance arrived _____ they were helping an injured man.
6. The police questioned the drivers _____ the paramedics were putting the injured man in the ambulance.
7. _____ they were writing their report, a tow truck arrived.
8. _____ the tow truck was moving the car, it started to rain.
9. _____ it started to rain, the police left.
10. We were standing in the rain _____ the bus arrived.

"Another," "Other," "Others"

Read the dialogue. Complete the dialogue with the adjectives **another** and **other** or the pronoun **others**.

Lost and Found

Man:	Excuse me. I left my raincoat on the plane. Do you have a raincoat there?
Airport Agent:	Which airline? Was it Air Canada?
Man:	No, it was _____ airline. It was KLM.
Airport Agent:	Were you on KLM 867 this morning?
Man:	No, it was one of their _____ flights.
Airport Agent:	Was it Flight 536 this afternoon?
Man:	Maybe, or maybe it was _____ one. Did you find a raincoat?
Airport Agent:	Yes, I have a blue raincoat here.
Man:	Do you have some _____? My coat is tan.
Airport Agent:	We have a tan coat. It's size 46.
Man:	That's not mine. Do you have _____ sizes?
Airport Agent:	Yes, we have some _____. What size is your coat?
Man:	It's size 40.
Airport Agent:	I have a 40 in blue. Oh wait, here are some _____ ones.
Man:	What do the _____ ones look like?
Airport Agent:	One's smaller than the _____. It's size 38.
Man:	Yes, I think that one is mine. Can I come and get it today, or is _____ day better?
Airport Agent:	No sir, come today. If it's not one of these coats, I'm sure it's _____ one.

Idioms

Use an idiomatic expression to replace the words in bold type in each sentence. Use the correct form of these expressions to help you.

to get through to	to go off
to give someone a minute	never mind
sharp	one of those things
to take off	

1. The train leaves at **exactly 5:00**. We should leave for the station now.
2. My alarm clock didn't **ring** this morning, so I was late for work.
3. I called Maria several times yesterday, but I couldn't **reach** her. The line was always busy.
4. I'm sorry I broke your glass. I didn't mean to. It was **just something that happened**.
5. This room is very messy. **Don't be concerned**, we can clean it up.
6. I'm almost ready to leave, but I can't find my keys. Just **wait** while I look for them.

7. Do you always **remove** your shoes at the front door?

8. I tried to reach my aunt yesterday, but I wasn't able to **reach** her. Maybe her telephone was out of order.

9. Come on in and **remove** your coat. I'll hang it up for you.

Score for Test Yourself: _____
50

Listening and Speaking: Using Idioms

What Happened to You?

C. Listen and write the missing words.

Tom: You're really late today Max. What happened to you? We were supposed to meet at 10:00 _____.

Max: I know, I know. I'm really sorry, Tom. My alarm didn't go _____, so I slept in.

Tom: Why didn't you call?

Max: I called you, but I couldn't get _____. The line was busy.

Tom: I know I was on the phone for a while, but it wasn't that long.

Max: Look, I said I was sorry. It's just one of those _____.

Tom: Never _____. Let's get started. We have a lot of work to do today.

Max: Okay. Just give me a minute to take my coat _____. Then we can get right to work.

D. Practise the dialogue with a partner.

E. Work with a partner. Write a dialogue about being late. Use as many idioms as you can.

8

"How much"/"How many"

Quantifiers

"Much," "Many," "A lot of"

"Little," "A little," "Few," "A few"

"No," "None," "None of"

Word Power

Work with a partner. Find these things in the picture:

an airline ticket   a suitcase   a camera   a travel brochure   money   a sun hat
suntan lotion   golf clubs   bathing suits   towels   a raincoat   sweaters   a purse
a surfboard   sunglasses   a palm tree   sunshine

Understanding Grammar

UNDERSTAND: **"How much"/"How many"**

Use **how much** to ask WH-information questions about quantity with non-count nouns. Use **how many** to ask WH-information questions about the number of things with count nouns.

Non-count   How **much luggage** do you have?

Count   How **many suitcases** do you have?

A. Complete the questions with **how much** or **how many**.

1. _____ miles is it between Amsterdam and Rome?
2. _____ money should I take with me?
3. _____ times do I have to change planes?
4. _____ bags can I take with me on the plane?
5. _____ hours difference is there between New York and Paris?
6. _____ meals are included in the price?
7. _____ time does it take to get a visa?
8. _____ swimming can I do at this time of year?
9. _____ luggage does the airline allow per passenger?
10. _____ sun can we expect to see while we are there?

B. Some sentences have errors. Find the errors and correct them.

1. How much dollars did that cost?
2. How many times did you phone the airline?
3. How much money did you bring with you?
4. How much tourists come here every year?
5. How many luggage did you have?
6. How much time did you spend in Hawaii?
7. How much rooms does the hotel have?
8. How much people took the flight?
9. How many sun is there in Cuba?
10. How much pesos is an American dollar worth?

a camera   a sun hat   golf clubs   a bathing suit   a surfboard   a palm tree

106

UNDERSTAND: **Count and Non-count**

A. Choose the correct noun form.

1. There is lots of **traffic/traffics** on the road.
2. I think we need more **information/informations**.
3. I can borrow **money/moneys** from my sister.
4. Did you leave your **luggage/luggages** in the trunk?
5. Our guide is the one with the blond **hair/hairs**.
6. The server brought me **a water/some water**.
7. Did you have a comfortable **travel/trip**?
8. Our hotel room has nice **furniture/furnitures**.
9. I hope we have **a good news/some good news** soon.
10. Why isn't there **a bread/any bread** on the table?

B. Match non-count nouns with similar count nouns.

1. travel   a) sweaters
2. furniture   b) storms
3. food   c) dollars
4. time   d) trips
5. weather   e) movies
6. clothing   f) suitcases
7. entertainment   g) hours
8. luggage   h) peanuts
9. money   i) buses
10. traffic   j) sofas

UNDERSTAND: **Quantifiers**

"Much," "Many," "A lot of"

Do not use **much** in affirmative statements. Use **a lot of**. The informal expression **lots of** means the same as **a lot of**. It is used in spoken and informal written English.

✗ We got **much** information from the travel agent.

✔ We got **a lot of** information from the travel agent.

a server   furniture   a storm   peanuts   a sofa   bread

Use **much** and **many** in negative statements.

We didn't see **many** tourists on the beach.

We didn't get **much** information from the tourist office.

A. Complete the sentences with **much** or **many** for negative sentences and **a lot of** for affirmative sentences

1. We met _____ people at the hotel.
2. We didn't play _____ golf because of bad weather.
3. The tour guide told us _____ interesting facts about the island.
4. The tornado in Miami caused _____ worry among the visitors.
5. Our trip to Mexico wasn't _____ fun because we lost our travellers' cheques.
6. The hotel offered _____ activities for evening entertainment.
7. We didn't see _____ museums in the towns we visited.
8. The hotel staff spoke _____ different languages.
9. The restaurant didn't offer _____ seafood on the menu.
10. The people we met in Brazil didn't speak _____ English.

> **TEACHER'S BOX:** Affirmative sentences use **many** rather than **a lot of** in formal usage.

B. Answer the questions with the short answer forms **not much**, **not many**, or **a lot**.

How much money does a taxi cost?   **a lot**

1. How much money does a bus ride cost?
2. How many people live in New York?
3. How much rain is there in Vancouver?
4. How much cold weather is there in Mexico?
5. How many people in the world speak Swedish?
6. How many people in the world speak Spanish?
7. How many volcanoes are there in Hawaii?
8. How many snow storms are there in Florida?
9. How much warm weather does Iceland have?
10. How many people ride bicycles in China?

a museum   seafood   a menu   a bicycle   a tornado   a volcano

"Little"/"a little," "Few"/"a few"

Use **little/a little** with non-count nouns.

> There is **little** rain in the desert.
>
> There is **a little** water in my glass.

Use **few/a few** with count nouns.

> **Few** plants can grow in the desert.
>
> **A few** palm trees grow near the oasis.

Little and **few** give a negative sense of quantity.

Non-count	They have **little** money.
Count	They have **few** friends.

A. Choose **little** or **few** to complete the sentences.

1. There are _____ places where you don't need money.
2. We have _____ time to waste before the sun sets.
3. There is _____ night life on an island like this.
4. The tourists saw _____ signs of life when they arrived.
5. The tour guide had _____ information about the ruins.
6. There was _____ fresh food on the menu.
7. The hotel had _____ rooms with private baths.
8. The group had _____ warning about the temperature.
9. The island had _____ facilities to offer visitors.
10. There were _____ servers in the restaurant at dinner time.

A little and **a few** give a positive sense of quantity.

Non-count	I can lend you **a little** money.
Count	I can introduce you to **a few** people.

B. Choose **a little** or **a few** to complete the sentences.

1. The first things we saw were _____ palm trees on the horizon.
2. When we arrived, there was _____ daylight, so we took pictures.
3. We noticed _____ people looking at us from across the room.
4. We paid only _____ dollars for these beautiful souvenirs.
5. The tourists tried to find _____ things to eat on the menu.

| plants | souvenirs | to pay | the horizon | an oasis | an island |

6. We asked the server to bring _____ water with the meal.

7. Everyone left _____ money as a tip for the server.

8. The tour guide took us to _____ interesting places the next day.

9. We had _____ time before we went to the hotel.

10. Our photos will give us _____ souvenirs of the trip.

"No," "None," "None of"

Use **no** before singular or plural nouns. Use **no** + noun to show the complete absence of something. Using **there are no** + noun is a strong way to say **there isn't any** or **there aren't any**.

There is**n't any** money.　　=　There is **no** money.

There are**n't any** apples.　　=　There are **no** apples.

Do not use a negative verb with **no** + noun.

✗ I don't have no money.

Use **none** as a pronoun to show the complete absence of something.

Is there any milk in the fridge? No, **none**.

How many restaurants are there in this hotel? **None**.

Use **none of** before determiners (**the, this, these**, etc.), possessive adjectives (**my, your, our**, etc.) and some object pronouns (**you, it, us, them**).

None of these were his.

None of his information was correct.

None of us trusts him after what happened.

Language in Transition

Noun phrases with **none of** can be followed by the plural verb form in informal, spoken English: **None of us speak Greek.** The singular form of the verb is used in formal language: **None of us speaks Greek.**

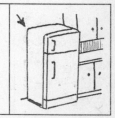

a warning　　　photos　　　a tour guide　　　a tip　　　milk　　　a refrigerator

A. Make these negative sentences stronger by using **no** + noun.

1. There isn't any sunshine today.
2. There isn't a server for this part of the dining room.
3. There aren't any blue raincoats in the lost and found.
4. There aren't any frequent flyer points on this route.
5. There aren't any lifeguards on duty at the swimming pool.
6. There aren't any surfboards for rent at this resort.
7. There aren't any tour guides available today.
8. There isn't a discount on the price here.
9. There aren't any problems with our accommodations.
10. There aren't any plans to return.

B. Use **no, none,** or **none of** to complete the sentences.

1. _____ the people we talked to were unhappy.
2. We received _____ warning about the tornado.
3. After the storm _____ us wanted to go to the beach.
4. _____ the tour guide's instructions were useful.
5. How much of the dessert did you eat? I ate _____.
6. We left so quickly there was _____ time to pack properly.
7. _____ the meals were included in the price of the hotel.
8. He paid _____ taxes before the police caught him.
9. _____ us believed what the salesman told us.
10. There was _____ news of our luggage, so we left the airport.

Listening and Speaking: Using Idioms

A Package Deal

A. Choose an expression that means the same as the words in bold type.

1. A trip to Europe can be expensive, but it is more reasonable with **a package deal**.

   a) a large cardboard box
   b) a plan with everything included
   c) a closed package

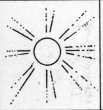   

| sunshine | a raincoat | a lifeguard | on duty | a salesman | dessert |

2. I am going to live in California for a year. I want a **one-way** ticket.
    a) a ticket that goes in one direction around the world
    b) a ticket to go somewhere together
    c) a ticket to go somewhere, but not to return

3. A **return** ticket is more expensive than a one-way ticket.
    a) a ticket to go somewhere and return home
    b) a ticket that allows to you travel several times
    c) a ticket that comes back to you after the trip

4. Raoul is a teacher. He works from September to June, but he has **time off** in the summer.
    a) a lot of time
    b) time away from work
    c) a short time

5. If we want to travel this summer, we have to **book** the tickets now.
    a) find the tickets
    b) reserve the tickets
    c) read the tickets

6. We need our tickets right away. I'll ask the travel agent to **make them out** today.
    a) prepare them
    b) make something new
    c) give them away

7. I reserved a movie for tonight. Can you go to the video store and **pick it up**?
    a) carry it
    b) get it
    c) lift it

8. My family can't decide where to go on holiday this year. We have to **talk it over**.
    a) speak loudly
    b) discuss it
    c) ask about it

9. I'm not sure about what I will do tomorrow. I'll **get back to** you when I have decided.
    a) go behind your back
    b) ask for something back
    c) contact you again

to pack   unhappy   a beach   taxes   police   to catch

B. Listen and answer the questions.

1. Where does the woman want to go?
2. Who is the woman travelling with?
3. When are the specials?
4. Why can't the woman travel before the end of June?
5. Why does the travel agent suggest that the woman book early?
6. What does the woman want to do before she books the tickets?

Turn to page 116 for Exercise C.

Ten-Minute Grammar Games

A Quantity Survey

Focus: Practise questions and answers with **how much, how many**.

The students use the items below to make questions with **how much** or **how many**.

How many magazines do you read every month?

How much coffee do you drink every day?

Then they each survey four students in the class. They ask the questions they have prepared and get as much information as they can for each one.

Name:				
1. books				
2. newspapers				
3. TV				
4. movies				
5. tapes/CDs				
6. sleep				
7. pairs of shoes				
8. snacks				
9. time travelling to class				
10. time talking on the phone				

What Could It Be?

Focus: Practise describing quantities.

Students put the missing word from each sentence in the puzzle. Then they find the secret question.

ice shampoo money lemon fish people honey sugar homework wine
water grapes mustard ice cream

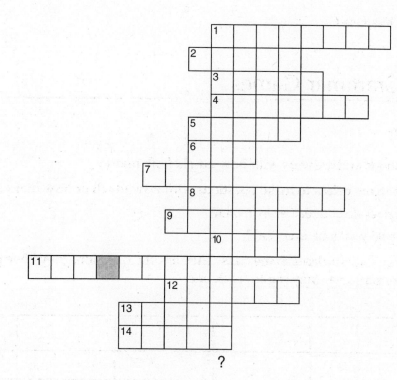

?

1. I have a whole lot of _____ to do for my class tomorrow.
2. There isn't a great deal of _____ in my wallet.
3. We'll be thirsty on the hike. Let's buy a bottle of _____ to take with us.
4. I'd like a bit of _____ to put on my sandwich.
5. The bowl is empty. There isn't a grain of _____ for my coffee.
6. I'd like a glass of cola please. Go easy on the _____.
7. There are tonnes of _____ in the ocean.
8. I want to wash my hair, but there isn't a drop of _____ left in the bottle.
9. The theatre is really crowded today. There are masses of _____ here.
10. We like to celebrate birthdays with a glass of _____.
11. Can I have another scoop of _____ for my cone, please.
12. Do you like fruit? Here is a bunch of _____.
13. Here is a slice of _____ for your tea.
14. Here is a bit of _____ for your bread.

Numbers and Words

Focus: Practise quantities and numbers.

Students write the words for each number or symbol.

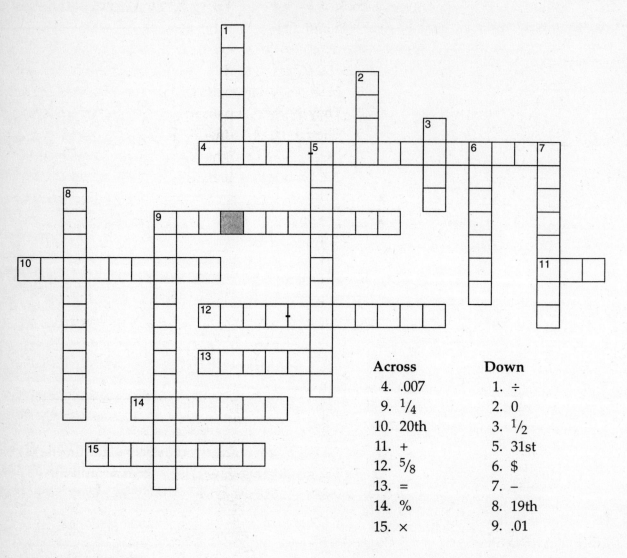

Across
4. .007
9. ¹/₄
10. 20th
11. +
12. ⁵/₈
13. =
14. %
15. ×

Down
1. ÷
2. 0
3. ¹/₂
5. 31st
6. $
7. −
8. 19th
9. .01

Test Yourself

"How much"/"How many"

Complete the sentences with **how much** or **how many**.

1. How _____ people live in your city?
2. How _____ butter do we need for that recipe?
3. How _____ snow do they have in winter?
4. How _____ friends do you still have from childhood?
5. How _____ difficulty do you have with English?
6. How _____ patience do teachers need?

7. How _____ information do you need before your trip?
8. How _____ trees are there on your street?
9. How _____ vitamin C do you need to take every day?
10. How _____ interesting facts did you learn during the lecture?

Quantifiers

A. Some sentences have errors. Find the errors and correct them.

1. Are much perfumes from France expensive?
2. Unfortunately, much popular movies are violent.
3. Does too many caffeine make people nervous?
4. A lot people like to gossip over the back fence.
5. I didn't sleep many on my holidays.
6. Did you have many rain last summer?
7. Did the students have many problems with the course?
8. We need to do a lot of shopping for the party.
9. Let's try to get a lot of exercise this weekend.
10. Are you sending much postcards from your holiday?

B. Choose **little**, **few**, **a little**, or **a few** to complete the sentences.

1. You will be happy to learn that there are _____ beaches near the hotel.
2. The handicraft market is only _____ minutes walk from the beach.
3. This map is useful because it gives _____ information about the island.
4. Luckily we learned that there are _____ mosquitoes near the ocean.
5. It is very dry around here because there is _____ rainfall at this time of year.
6. Please call the server and ask for _____ ice with our tea.
7. We don't need a map because there are _____ streets to follow.
8. Let's go to the post office. I have _____ postcards to send to people at home.
9. Let's all go to the swimming pool and get _____ exercise before dinner.
10. You should take some photos soon because there are only _____ hours of daylight left.

C. Complete the sentences with **no**, **none of**, or **none**.

1. There is _____ milk left in the refrigerator.
2. _____ the appliances in this apartment work.
3. Have you been to any baseball games this season? No, _____.
4. _____ the people on the bus tour knew each other.
5. I asked a lot of people for the answer, but I got _____ response.
6. We took a lot of photographs, but _____ them are very good.
7. I could find _____ mistakes in their compositions.
8. I have absolutely no doubt about the car I want to buy, _____ at all.
9. There was _____ time left, so we had to give our assignment in.
10. Robert usually takes _____ sugar in his coffee.

116

Idioms

Complete the paragraph using the correct form of the idioms below.

to talk it over	one-way ticket	a package deal
time off	to pick up	a return ticket
to book a ticket	to make out a ticket	to get back to someone

Mauricio is taking a trip to Paris this summer. The summer is a good time to travel because Mauricio has _____ off from his classes. He _____ his ticket last week. At first, the travel agent suggested a _____ deal because it was less expensive that way, but Mauricio wanted to _____ it over with his family.

Finally Mauricio decided to buy a _____ ticket, because he wasn't sure how long he would stay. He knew that he could always get a _____ ticket later. He asked the travel agent to _____ out the ticket for June 15, because he wanted to _____ the ticket early. Mauricio's friend called to ask for information about the trip. Mauricio told her that he would find out if there were still tickets available, and would get _____ her right away. He suggested that if she wanted to go, she should also _____ her ticket early.

Score for Test Yourself: _____
50

Listening and Speaking: Using Idioms

A Package Deal

C. Listen and write the words.

Travel agent: Can I help you?

Woman: Yes, I'd like to go to Mexico on holiday. How much will it cost?

Travel agent: That depends on what you want. Do you want a package _____?

Woman: No, I'm travelling with my friend. We don't want to travel in a group.

Travel agent: Okay. Is that one _____ or return?

Woman: It's _____. Do you have any specials?

Travel agent: Yes, we have some special rates in April.

Woman: No, that's no good. I don't have any time _____ until the end of June.

Travel agent: Well, July is a busy month. I suggest you _____ early. If you book this week I can make _____ the tickets, and you can pick them _____ next Friday.

Woman: Well, I'm not sure. I want to talk it _____ with my friend. When I make up my mind, I'll get _____ to you.

D. Practise the conversation with a partner.

E. Work with a partner. Write a dialogue about booking tickets for a vacation. Use as many idioms as you can.

9

Gerunds
Reflexive Pronouns
Irregular Plural Nouns

Reflexive Pronouns

myself
yourself
himself
herself
itself

ourselves
yourselves
themselves

Irregular Plural Forms

man	men
woman	women
child	children
person	people
foot	feet
tooth	teeth
goose	geese
mouse	mice
half	halves
knife	knives
leaf	leaves
life	lives
thief	thieves
wife	wives

Word Power

Work with a partner. Match the words to the pictures.

watch TV   **overeat**   **swim**   **exercise**   **relax**   **lift weights**   **smoke**   **jog**   **lie in the sun**

Understanding Grammar

UNDERSTAND: **Gerunds**

A gerund is made from a verb, but it functions as a noun. A gerund can function as the subject or object of a sentence. It can also function as the object of a preposition.

Subject	**Swimming** is good for you.
Object	We like **swimming**.
Object of a preposition	He is interested in **swimming**.

A gerund is made with the present participle form of the verb (**ing** form *without* the auxiliary verb **be**). Look at the examples of a noun and a gerund.

Noun	**Cigarettes** are bad for you.
Gerund	**Smoking** is bad for you.

Note: The verb **go** + gerund is often used to describe sports and activities: **go camping, go skiing, go dancing, go jogging, go shopping.**

TEACHER'S BOX: Rules about the use of gerunds following certain verbs (gerunds vs. infinitives) are found in *Grammar Connections 3*. The focus of the activities here is gerunds as nouns in subject or object position.

A. Find the subject in each sentence. Match the subjects to the gerunds.

1.	Books give interesting information.	a)	lying down
2.	Exercise is good for you.	b)	drawing
3.	Humour makes people laugh.	c)	swimming
4.	Cigarettes are dangerous for you.	d)	reading
5.	Weights build strong muscles.	e)	body building
6.	Silence is golden.	f)	dancing
7.	Ballet develops the muscles.	g)	keeping quiet
8.	Art develops the mind.	h)	smoking
9.	Rest helps relax the body.	i)	telling jokes
10.	TV can be educational for children.	j)	watching TV

muscles	to build	body building	ballet	to lie down	to laugh

B. Find the gerunds.

1. Walking to work is a good way to get exercise.
2. Everyone knows that smoking is bad for your lungs.
3. Jogging is good for your heart.
4. Breathing fresh air makes us feel good.
5. You can stay fit by exercising often.
6. We always feel better after getting enough sleep.
7. One way to damage your skin is by sunbathing.
8. Watching too much TV is a bad habit.
9. Eating too much can make people fat.
10. Try swimming or playing tennis if you want exercise.

C. Find the prepositions. Then complete the sentences with the gerund form of the verbs below.

cook   walk   forget   play   say   bring   see   drive   shop   wear

1. They are tired of _____ for clothes.
2. We should thank Bob for _____ us home.
3. Max is really good at _____ Chinese food
4. Jenna is worried about _____ my telephone number.
5. Is anyone interested in _____ tennis?
6. Everyone is excited about _____ the concert.
7. Did you think about _____ something to drink?
8. Let's not leave without _____ goodbye.
9. Don't sit in the sun without _____ sunscreen.
10. Susanna is afraid of _____ home alone at night.

UNDERSTAND: **Spelling the Gerund Form**

When the base form of the verb ends with **e**, drop the **e** before adding **ing**.

wave   waving

When the syllable that is stressed ends in one vowel and one consonant, double the consonant before adding **ing** to the base form of the verb.

stop   stopping
begin   beginning

TEACHER'S BOX: Failure to double the final consonant would result in changes to the pronunciation of the preceding vowel. For example, **planning** would be pronounced **planing** (plane-ing).

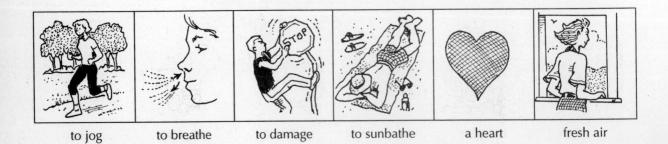

to jog   to breathe   to damage   to sunbathe   a heart   fresh air

A. Write the gerund form of these verbs.

1. ask	8. forget	15. camp
2. swim	9. jog	16. smoke
3. play	10. eat	17. skate
4. watch	11. try	18. ski
5. sit	12. ride	19. get
6. stop	13. shop	20. hit
7. run	14. plan	

B. Some sentences have spelling errors in the gerunds. Find the errors and correct them.

1. Studying late makes a person tired the next day.
2. Siting in the sun can be dangerous for the health.
3. One sport I really enjoy is rideing a mountain bike.
4. We went campping in the mountains last summer.
5. Joging is a sport that people practise in many cities.
6. The tourists usually go swiming at that beach in the morning.
7. I don't really enjoy sitting on the beach in the sun.
8. The bus driver irritated us by stoping too often.
9. Cooking with oil is not always a healthy way to prepare food.
10. Forgeting my camera was the worst experience of my trip.

UNDERSTAND: **Reflexive Pronouns**

Use a reflexive pronoun when the subject and object of a sentence are the same person.

The young **boy** dressed **himself.**

Use reflexive pronouns with **by** to mean **alone**.

I found the address **by myself.**

We built this table **by ourselves.**

> **TEACHER'S BOX:** Activities that are normally done alone, such as washing, shaving, combing your hair, etc, are **not** used with reflexive pronouns in English:
>
> ✗ He shaved himself.   ✔ He shaved.

| to swim | to camp | mountains | a beach | to plan | oil |

Reflexive pronouns have the singular ending **self** or the plural ending **selves**.

> myself
> yourself
> himself
> herself
> itself
>
> ourselves
> yourselves
> themselves

TEACHER'S BOX: Because the rules for forming reflexive pronouns are idiosyncratic, students often assume forms such as hisself or theirselves, which are logical but incorrect.

A. Write the correct form of the reflexive pronouns.

Annabel   herself

1. all the players
2. my sister and I
3. my best friend
4. my team
5. the dog

6. everyone here
7. that lady
8. my brother
9. you alone
10. you and your team

B. Use reflexive pronouns to complete the sentences.

1. I was alone at the party so I introduced _____.
2. John wasn't bored because he knew how to amuse _____.
3. The spectators protected _____ from the rain with umbrellas.
4. The cat got up and stretched _____.
5. Some people can teach _____ to do sports.
6. Maybe you can teach _____ to play tennis.
7. Why don't you all help _____ to coffee?
8. Maria excused _____ and left the locker room.
9. The guests served _____ from the buffet.
10. I heard that people enjoyed _____ at the game.

spectators   to protect   to stretch   guests   buffet   alone

C. Complete the sentences. Use **by** + a reflexive pronoun to replace the word **alone**.

Cooking healthy meals is something you can do alone.   **by yourself**

1. Jogging is a sport that people often do alone.
2. Thank you, but I can open the door alone.
3. Don't try to carry all that equipment alone.
4. The man found the door to the gym alone.
5. Anna prepared for the tennis match alone.
6. The coach let us choose partners alone.
7. The stadium doors seemed to open alone.
8. You can't play badminton very well alone.
9. We planned the party for after the game alone.
10. Janet set up all the equipment for the game alone.

UNDERSTAND: **Irregular Plural Forms**

Most nouns form the plural by adding **s** or **es**. A few nouns have irregular plural forms.

man	men
woman	women
child	children
person	people
foot	feet
tooth	teeth
goose	geese
mouse	mice

Some nouns form the plural as follows:

half	halves
knife	knives
leaf	leaves
life	lives
thief	thieves
wife	wives

TEACHER'S BOX: See Appendix 1, page 210 for the rules for spelling noun plurals.

a gym   a tennis match   a coach   a stadium   badminton   a goose

A. Write the plurals of these nouns.

1. spoon	8. window	15. fork
2. knife	9. life	16. person
3. house	10. goose	17. foot
4. child	11. animal	18. half
5. husband	12. woman	19. plates
6. wife	13. mouse	20. thief
7. tooth	14. leaf	

B. Some sentences have errors. Find the errors and correct them.

1. That family has three childrens.
2. They eat with knifes and forks.
3. Mouses are small animals.
4. We lived in three different houses.
5. Dentists take care of our tooths.
6. Some peoples are lazier than others.
7. Some thiefs robbed the bank in town.
8. The brothers went on holiday with their wifes.
9. They say a cat has nine lives.
10. Two people came to our door today.

> **Language in Transition**
>
> In the past the common plural form for **person** was **persons**. It is still correct, but the form we commonly use today is **people**.

Listening and Speaking: Using Idioms

Welcome to the Party

A. Study the expressions used in the sentences.

1. Welcome to my house. Come in and **make yourself at home**.
2. Some of the people at the party are in our class. We know **quite a few** people.
3. You can **introduce yourself** to the people that you don't know.
4. There is some food on the table. Please **help yourself**.
5. Chen is **good at** cooking. He made all the food himself.
6. Paul is late, **as usual**. He is late for everything.
7. I studied hard for the exam, and it really **made a difference**.

| a spoon | a knife | a fork | a mouse | lazy | to rob |

B. Match the expressions on the left to the meanings on the right.

1. to make yourself at home   a) to affect
2. quite a few   b) as is typical, as often happens
3. to introduce yourself   c) to make yourself comfortable
4. to help yourself to something   d) to do something well
5. to be good at   e) to take something
6. as usual   f) to meet other people
7. to make a difference   g) several, many

C. Listen and write **T** (true) or **F** (false) for each statement.

1. Lili and Yumi are at a party.
2. Yumi doesn't know anyone at the party.
3. Lili and Chen bought the food.
4. Chen is good at making dessert.

Turn to page 129 for Exercise D.

Ten-Minute Grammar Games

Sentence Ends

Focus: Practise using gerunds after prepositions.

Students choose five beginnings from the list below. They finish each sentence by writing something interesting or unusual about themselves. They must use a gerund after the preposition. They write their sentences on a piece of paper, without writing their names.

Students then work in groups. They put their papers in a pile. Then they take turns selecting a paper and reading the sentences aloud. Students guess who the writer is. After they guess correctly, they can ask the writer questions to find out more about each idea.

1. I'm looking forward to…
2. I'm planning on…
3. I'm happy about…
4. I'm worried about…
5. I'm afraid of…
6. I'm interested in…
7. I'm good at…
8. I'm tired of…

What Is It?

Focus: Practise reflexive pronouns.

Across

3. Babies can't do this by themselves.
4. Some people admire themselves when they look in these.
7. People protect themselves with this when it rains.
9. People usually do this form of exercise by themselves.
10. We enjoy ourselves when we go to one of these.
12. Men do this by themselves every morning.
13. We wash ourselves with this.
15. People can't play this sport by themselves.

Down

1. People keep themselves warm with these.
2. We dry ourselves with this.
4. People blame themselves when they make these.
5. A child can cut himself or herself with these.
6. Students usually do this by themselves.
8. We can teach ourselves new things with these.
11. People make these for themselves when they are hungry.
14. Cooks can hurt themselves if they are not careful with these.

Bumping Words

Focus: Practise gerunds.

Each box contains four words. Three of the words are similar. The word that is different should be "bumped" out to the next box. The next box will also contain three similar words, and one word that does not fit.

Students continue bumping the words until they reach the end. The last box contains one word that does not fit. They use that word to complete the sentence at the bottom. The first box is done as an example.

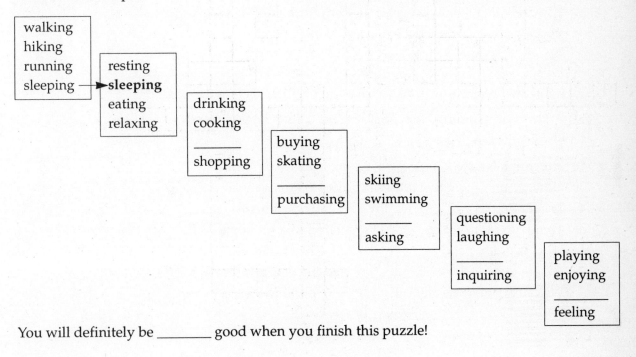

You will definitely be _____ good when you finish this puzzle!

Test Yourself

Gerunds

A. Use the gerund form of the verbs.

exercise   smoke   walk   overeat   do   camp   raise   swim   jog   sit

1. **Something** children is an important responsibility.
2. **Something** causes people to gain weight.
3. Many people are afraid of **something** in the ocean.
4. They don't like **something** because of the mosquitos.
5. **Something** alone at night in a big city can be dangerous.
6. **Something** aerobics can be very good for your health.
7. Doctors advise against cigarettes and **something**.
8. **Something** in the sun can cause skin cancer.
9. A good way to get exercise in the park is **something**.
10. **Something** daily is a good way to stay fit.

B. Some sentences have errors. Find the errors and correct them.

1. They like to go swim in the summer.
2. You can lose weight by exercising.
3. Eat well is good for everyone's health.
4. Smoke cigarettes is a very bad habit.
5. We went camping in the mountains last year.
6. Arrive late at work is not a good idea.
7. A vegetarian doesn't believe in eat meat.
8. John isn't in the office because he went fishing.
9. Maria really enjoys ride a bicycle to work.
10. We can go skate by ourselves.

C. Complete the sentences with the correct prepositions before the gerunds.

from   to   of   about   for   before   at   in   after   over

1. Let's have coffee _____ going to class.
2. Are you interested _____ seeing a movie on Friday?
3. How _____ going for dinner after the movie?
4. We are thinking _____ inviting Anne to join us.
5. Thank you very much _____ giving us a lift home.
6. Marc is pretty good _____ fixing a computer.
7. We are looking forward _____ seeing you again soon.
8. We can go to the restaurant _____ parking the car.
9. We are tired _____ skiing all weekend.
10. They chose tennis _____ playing soccer.

Reflexive Pronouns

Some sentences have errors. Find the errors and correct them.

1. Charlie hurt hisself while playing soccer.
2. Listen guys, exercise is a good way to keep yourself fit.
3. Karen accidentally cut herself with a knife.
4. The kids didn't know how to dress theirselves.
5. I made this entire delicious meal by myself.
6. The teacher invited us to talk about ourself.
7. Please come in and make yourselfs at home.
8. Dan stepped forward and helped hisself to a piece of cake.
9. We all introduced ourselves before the class.
10. Please tell me something interesting about yourself.

Idioms

Fill in each blank with an appropriate idiom. Use the correct form of these idioms to help you.

to make yourself at home
quite a few
to introduce yourself
to help yourself to something
to be good at
as usual
to make a difference

1. I like music, but I don't have a good voice, so I'm not very _____ singing.
2. The buses are always slow on a rainy day. It's raining hard now, so I guess they will be late, _____.
3. A lot of people are sick this week. _____ students were absent from class today.
4. The work on this project is excellent. Your extra effort really _____.
5. When you go to a new class, it's a good idea to _____ to a few people.
6. I brought some food for lunch today. If you are hungry, just _____.
7. You are always welcome in my house. Come in and _____ at home.
8. I _____ to _____ people at the meeting last night.
9. Our meetings always start late. This one is starting late too, _____.

Score for Test Yourself: _____
50

Listening and Speaking: Using Idioms

Welcome to the Party

D. Listen and write the missing words.

Lili: Hi Yumi. Welcome to the party. Come on in. Make _____ at home.

Yumi: Thanks Lili. Everything looks great. I always look forward to your parties.

Lili: Let me introduce you to some people.

Yumi: That's okay. I know _____ a few people here. I can introduce _____ to the others.

Lili: Okay. Please help _____ to some food.

Yumi: Did you and Chen make all this food _____?

Lili: Most of it. I made the main courses. Chen is very _____ at making desserts.

Yumi: Everything looks delicious, as _____. It really makes a _____ when you prepare everything yourselves.

130

E. Practise the conversation with a partner.

F. Write a dialogue about a party. Use as many idioms as you can.

10 Review Unit

Dining Out With Fiona

A. Read the restaurant review and answer the questions.

Aux Deux Gauloises is a restaurant that I can heartily recommend. My companion and I had an excellent meal there last Friday evening. We sat down at the table and the server arrived immediately with a basket of bread, glasses of water, and the menu. My companion asked for ice in his water, and we looked over the menu.

For appetizers we chose a fish soup and a fresh green salad. I asked the server to bring some butter for my bread when he brought the appetizers. My salad tasted wonderful and my friend's soup smelled delicious.

Our main course was poultry. I chose roast duck and my companion ordered Chicken Basquaise. When he was asked, the server told my friend that the Basquaise sauce was made from tomatoes, green peppers, and spices. My duck was tender and was served with an excellent sauce.

My friend didn't want dessert but I ordered chocolate mousse. The server asked if I would like the dessert with whipped cream. I decided to skip the whipped cream. Both of us ended the meal with coffee.

When the bill came, the server asked how we would like to pay. I paid cash and asked for a receipt, which came immediately. It was a very pleasant evening and I will be sure to go to Aux Deux Gauloises again.

1. When did Fiona go to the restaurant?
2. What did the server bring to the table?
3. What did Fiona's companion ask for?

4. What did Fiona ask the waiter to bring with the appetizers?
5. What did Fiona and her friend order as the main course?
6. How did they find out what was in the Basquaise sauce?
7. Why didn't her friend have dessert?
8. What did the server ask Fiona about her dessert?
9. What was the last thing that they ordered?
10. What did Fiona ask for when she paid the bill?

B. Work in pairs to complete the dialogue. Replace the expressions in brackets with polite requests using **could**, **would**, or **may**. Add **please** where appropriate. Then practise the dialogue with your partner.

Server: Good evening. Are you ready to order?

Diner 1: We're not ready yet. _____ (come back) later.

Diner 2: _____ (give me) a glass of water, and _____ (put) ice in it.

Server: Can I take your orders now?

Diner 1: _____ (I want) a green salad and roast duck. _____ (give me) some butter with the bread.

Diner 2: _____ (give me) the fish soup and the Chicken Basquaise.

Server: _____ (do you want) any dessert?

Diner 2: No, thank you. _____ (just bring me) some coffee.

Diner 1: _____ (I want) the chocolate mousse.

Server: _____ (do you want) whipped cream with the mousse?

Diner 1: Yes, please, and _____ (bring) me some coffee too?

C. Work in pairs. Write a dialogue. Order the items on the waiter's notepad using polite expressions.

1 soup	2 cheese cake
1 salad	1 coffee
salmon	1 tea
roast veal	
1 soda water	
1 water (no ice)	

The Police Report

A. Look at the picture and answer the police officer's questions. Use short answers.

1. Who was driving the car that hit the telephone pole?
2. How many people were riding in the car?
3. Who was standing in a good position to see the accident?
4. What was the truck doing when it cut off the car?
5. Who was driving the truck?
6. How many people were waiting at the bus stop?
7. What was the driver of the car doing when the police arrived?
8. What was the truck driver doing when the police arrived?
9. What was the woman passenger doing when the police arrived?
10. What was Mrs. Cook doing when the police arrived?

B. Use a sheet of paper. Write a police report describing what you found at the scene of the accident.

The Doctor's Advice

Read the labels on the medicines. Answer **T** (true) or **F** (false) to the following statements. Correct information that is false.

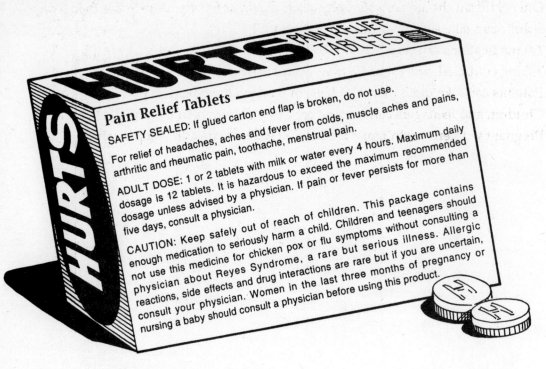

Pain Relief Tablets

SAFETY SEALED: If glued carton end flap is broken, do not use.

For relief of headaches, aches and fever from colds, muscle aches and pains, arthritic and rheumatic pain, toothache, menstrual pain.

ADULT DOSE: 1 or 2 tablets with milk or water every 4 hours. Maximum daily dosage is 12 tablets. It is hazardous to exceed the maximum recommended dosage unless advised by a physician. If pain or fever persists for more than five days, consult a physician.

CAUTION: Keep safely out of reach of children. This package contains enough medication to seriously harm a child. Children and teenagers should not use this medicine for chicken pox or flu symptoms without consulting a physician about Reyes Syndrome, a rare but serious illness. Allergic reactions, side effects and drug interactions are rare but if you are uncertain, consult your physician. Women in the last three months of pregnancy or nursing a baby should consult a physician before using this product.

Cold Medicine

FOR RELIEF OF COLD/FLU SYMPTOMS

Relieves sniffles and sneezing, calms and quiets coughing, eases head and body aches, relieves nasal and sinus congestion, reduces fever, relieves minor sore throat pain.

DOSAGE: Adults (ages 12 and over) take one capsule every 12 hours.

CAUTION: Do not exceed recommended dosage. Do not take this product for more than 7 days. Consult a physician if symptoms do not improve or are accompanied by high fever, or if cough worsens. Children under 12, elderly persons, pregnant or nursing women, persons with high blood pressure, thyroid problems, chronic lung disease or shortness of breath, heart disease, diabetes, glaucoma, depression, prostate gland enlargement, asthma, or persons under treatment for depression or using anti-depressant medications should use only under the direction of a physician.

May cause marked drowsiness. Alcohol may increase the drowsiness effect. Avoid alcoholic beverages. Do not drive or engage in activities requiring alertness until response is determined. As with any drug, if pregnant or nursing a baby, consult a health professional before using this product.

KEEP THIS AND ALL DRUGS OUT OF REACH OF CHILDREN. THIS PACKAGE CONTAINS ENOUGH MEDICINE TO SERIOUSLY HARM A CHILD.

1. You should take pain relief tablets with milk or water.
2. Everyone can take cold medicine.
3. Driving while taking cold medicine is safe.
4. Only children should consult a physician if pain or fever persists more than 5 days.
5. Adults can take a cold capsule every 4 hours.
6. All medications can seriously harm children.
7. Taking cold medicine for more than 7 days is not recommended.
8. Patients can take more than 12 tablets of pain relief medicine if they feel very sick.
9. Children and teenagers can become seriously ill from taking pain relief tablets.
10. Pregnant women mustn't take medication without consulting a physician.

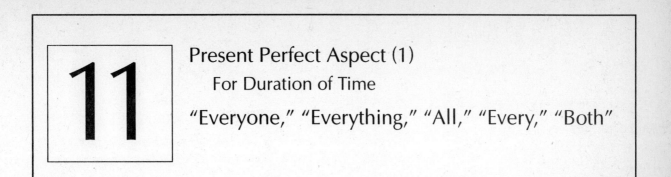

11   Present Perfect Aspect (1)
For Duration of Time
"Everyone," "Everything," "All," "Every," "Both"

Present Perfect Aspect: Duration of Time

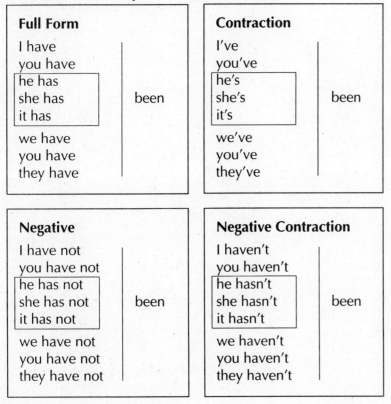

Full Form

I have
you have
| he has |
| she has | been
| it has |
we have
you have
they have

Contraction

I've
you've
| he's |
| she's | been
| it's |
we've
you've
they've

Negative

I have not
you have not
| he has not |
| she has not | been
| it has not |
we have not
you have not
they have not

Negative Contraction

I haven't
you haven't
| he hasn't |
| she hasn't | been
| it hasn't |
we haven't
you haven't
they haven't

Past Participles

Base form	Past tense	Past participle
be	was, were	been
go	went	gone (to school)
have	had	had
know	knew	known
live	lived	lived
speak	spoke	spoken (a language)
work	worked	worked

Word Power

Look at the picture. With a partner, describe what you see. Find people doing these activities:

neighbours talking	repairing a fence	riding a bicycle
mowing the lawn	painting a house	shaking a rug
gardening	playing ball	watering the lawn
raking leaves	putting out the garbage	walking a dog

Understanding Grammar

UNDERSTAND: **Present Perfect Aspect for Duration of Time**

Use the present perfect aspect for an action that began in the past and continues in the present.

> Do you live in Paris?
>
> Yes, we have lived in Paris for three years (**and we still do**).

Use the auxiliary verb **have** and the past participle of the main verb to form the present perfect.

> She **has lived** in Paris for three years.

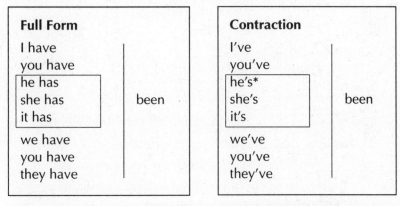

Full Form		Contraction	
I have		I've	
you have		you've	
he has		he's*	
she has	been	she's	been
it has		it's	
we have		we've	
you have		you've	
they have		they've	

* The **contraction** of the third person singular (**he**, **she**, **it**) forms of the present continuous and the present perfect are the same. You can recognize the present perfect because the auxiliary contraction is followed by the past participle.

> **TEACHER'S BOX:** It is more common to use the present perfect continuous than the present perfect to focus on duration of time, except with certain verbs such as **live, work, be, have, know,** and **speak (a language)**. See *Grammar Connections 3* for the present perfect continuous.

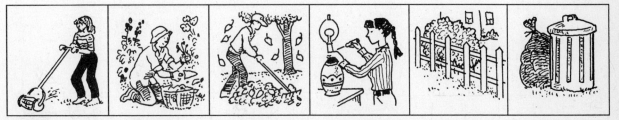

| to mow | to garden | to rake | to repair | a fence | garbage |

Verbs that occur in the present perfect for duration of time have both regular and irregular past participle forms. The regular form of the past participle is the same as the simple past tense (add **ed**). Some irregular past participle forms commonly used for duration of time from then until now are:

Base form	Past tense	Past participle
be	was, were	**been**
go	went	**gone** (to school)
have	had	**had**
know	knew	**known**
live	lived	**lived**
speak	spoke	**spoken** (a language)
work	worked	**worked**

See Appendix 2, page 211 for a full list of irregular past participle forms.

A. Complete the sentences with the present perfect form of one of the verbs in the chart above.

1. The Smiths and the Tremblays _____ neighbours for fifteen years.

2. Min Hee _____ English since she spent her summer vacation in Vancouver.

3. Sam and Carla _____ in the same office since the company opened.

4. Max and I _____ to the same school since we were in grade three.

5. Ping _____ the head librarian at the college for six years.

6. Mrs. McGregor _____ in the house next door since I was a child.

7. The Smith family next door _____ the same car for many years.

8. George Simpson _____ in an engineering office ever since he graduated university.

9. Lily Lee _____ Sam Woolens since elementary school.

10. Francesca _____ to the same language school since last year.

B. Look at the examples. Then choose the correct form of the verb for each sentence in the exercise.

Do you live in Paris?

No, **we lived** in Paris for three years, but we don't live there now.
(**Simple past**: the action was completed in past time.)

Yes, **we have lived** in Paris for six years.
(**Present perfect**: the action began in the past and continues in the present.)

neighbours   a librarian   a company   next door   to graduate   to live

1. Jane Green _____ (live) in the apartment next door before she got married.
2. Robert White _____ (live) in Houston since he got a job with the oil company.
3. My friend Geoff _____ (speak) Japanese since he lived in Japan as an English teacher.
4. Elizabeth _____ (speak) French to the travel agent in Switzerland.
5. Jane and Ben _____ (be) students at this college for about three years now.
6. Michael _____ (be) a police officer since he graduated from college last year.
7. Susanna _____ (be) a lawyer before she became my business partner.
8. John _____ (know) Dr. Han since they played in the same orchestra.
9. Carolyn _____ (know) my uncle when they were students at the same college.
10. No one on the team _____ (have) an accident this year.

UNDERSTAND: *"For" and "Since"*

Use **for** with the present perfect to focus on **a period of time** that continues to the present.

> We have been friends **for six years** (and we are still friends now).

Use **since** with the present perfect to focus on **the point in past time** when an action that continues first began.

> We have been friends **since 1990** (and we are still friends today).

TEACHER'S BOX: Students may have trouble with the notion that **since** refers to a point of time in the past. They may not see a difference between the idea of **since** 1988 and **for** 7 years (since 7 years ago).

A. Choose **for** or **since** to complete the sentences.

1. That building has been there _____ two years.
2. Those neighbours have lived next door to us _____ 1978.
3. They have been in the same class _____ last September.
4. The drugstore has had a sale on shampoo _____ three days.
5. My father has spoken Italian _____ he studied art in Florence.
6. Our parents have known each other _____ they were at college.
7. Joan and Tim have been happily married _____ nearly 16 years.
8. Audrey has been on vacation _____ almost three weeks now.
9. The man next door has worked for the city _____ many years.
10. The road has been closed for repairs _____ last Tuesday.

to get married	a police officer	to play music	an orchestra	a drugstore	shampoo

B. Complete the sentences in your own words.

1. We have lived in the same house for…
2. Frank has worked for the same company since…
3. Mei has lived in Toronto for…
4. Miguel has spoken English for…
5. Max and Mollie have known each other since…
6. Caroline has had a cold since…
7. Her parents have been married since…
8. We have known those people for…
9. Gabrielle has lived in Jakarta for…
10. She has been tired since…

UNDERSTAND: **Present Perfect Questions Related to Duration of Time**

When questions use the present perfect to refer to **duration of time**, the expression **long** or **how long** is often used. NB: **Long** does not refer to distance but to time here.

Have you been here long?   No, just 10 minutes.

How long have you lived in Vancouver?   (for) 5 years

A. Read the sentences. Write questions to help you get more information. Use **how long** and the present perfect.

Jun is a student. **How long has Jun been a student?**

1. Jun lives in Toronto.
2. He goes to a technical college.
3. Jun's uncle and aunt have a grocery store.
4. Jun works in the store on weekends.
5. He knows a young woman from New York.
6. They are in the same classes.
7. She speaks Korean.
8. Her family lives in New York.
9. She works in the library after school.
10. Jun and the young woman are good friends.

a cold

tired

a grocery store

the weekend

aunt   uncle

B. Read the sentences about a job interview. Put the sentences in the correct order. Write out the dialogue on a sheet of paper. The first two sentences are done for you.

Interviewer: Please sit down. I see you have a Seattle address.

Interviewee: Yes, I do.

1. No I haven't.
2. How long have you lived in Seattle?
3. Where do you work currently?
4. How long have you worked there?
5. I work at Boeing in the engineering department.
6. I moved here 15 years ago.
7. I've worked there for 10 years.
8. Have you always worked in the engineering department?
9. For 3 years.
10. How long have you worked in the engineering department?

UNDERSTAND: **Present Perfect Negative Related to Duration of Time**

The most common uses of the present perfect negative when it is related to duration of time are for **short answer form in denials**:

Have you worked here long? **No, I haven't.**

Or for **contradictions**:

She hasn't lived in New York for three years. She has lived there for two years.

Add **not** after the auxiliary verb **have** to form the negative. Use the contraction (**hasn't** or **haven't**) in spoken or informal written English.

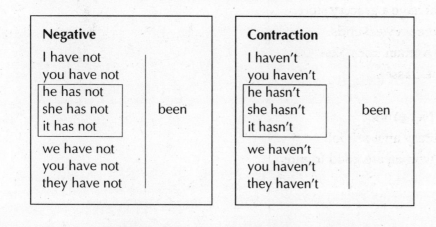

Negative		
I have not		
you have not		
he has not	been	
she has not		
it has not		
we have not		
you have not		
they have not		

Contraction		
I haven't		
you haven't		
he hasn't	been	
she hasn't		
it hasn't		
we haven't		
you haven't		
they haven't		

| an interview | to move | an engineer | an aircraft | an office | an address |

A. Use the information in the paragraph to complete the chart.

Number of years ago	Event
20	moved to Seattle
15	
12	
11	
10	
9	
7	
8	

Steve and Anita have been our neighbours for 8 years. Steve Carter move to Seattle from Calgary 20 years ago. He had a diploma as an aircraft technician, and he found work with a small company. Five years later he met a woman named Anita Woods. They were married 3 years later. Anita found a job as a accountant at Boeing the next year. Steve applied for a job at Boeing and one year later he was hired there too. The year after Steve began to work at Boeing, he and Anita had a baby boy. Two years later they had a girl. The year their daughter was born, the Carters bought a new car. A year later year they bought a house in the suburbs. We have been friends with Steve and Anita since the time they moved in.

B. Look at the chart. Correct the information in the sentences according to the information given in the chart.

They have been our neighbours for 10 years.

They haven't been our neighbours for 10 years. They've only been our neighbours for 8 years.

> **TEACHER'S BOX:** The intensifier **only** is frequently used in contradictions or denials that relate to duration of time: **He hasn't been here for an hour. He's only been here for 20 minutes** or **Have you been here long? No, I've only been here for a few minutes.**

1. Steve has lived in Seattle for 25 years.
2. Steve has known Anita for 18 years.
3. Steve and Anita have been married for 15 years.
4. Anita has worked for Boeing for 12 years.

a diploma   a technician   an accountant   a bride   a groom   a ring

5. Steve has worked at Boeing for longer that Anita has.
6. The Carters have been parents for 12 years.
7. The Carters have had a daughter longer than they have had a son.
8. Steve and Anita have had a car for 15 years.
9. The Carter family has lived in the suburbs for 10 years.
10. Steve and Anita have been friends with their neighbours for 10 years.

UNDERSTAND: *"Everyone," "Everything," "All," "Every," "Both"*

These words give information about **how many** people or things you are talking about.

Everyone or **everything** refers to people or things in general.

> **Everyone** likes music.

> **Everything** is all right.

All + plural noun refers to a specific group of people or things.

> **All** passengers must have boarding passes.

> **All** suitcases must be checked at security.

Every + singular noun has a similar meaning to **all**. **Every** focuses on the individual members of a specific group.

> **Every** passenger must have a boarding pass.

> **Every** suitcase must be checked at security.

Both + plural noun refers to two people or things.

> **Both** pilots wore uniforms.

> **Both** suitcases were lost.

A. Choose the best word to complete the conversations.

1. Who usually cuts the neighbours' grass, the husband or the wife?
   Usually they work together. They _____ cut the grass.

2. Which passengers have to show their passports at the border?
   _____ passengers are required to show their passports.

3. Who is going to come to the party on Saturday?
   I heard that _____ is going to be there.

4. Which children need love?
   That's a strange question. _____ children need love.

| the suburbs | a boarding pass | suitcases | security | a pilot | passengers |

5. Which car do you want to take to the party, mine or yours?
   Six of our friends want a lift. Let's take _____ cars.

6. Who gave the best presentation in class today, Sue or Sally?
   It's hard to say. _____ presentations were excellent.

7. Was anyone absent for the English test on Wednesday?
   No. The teacher said that _____ was there.

8. Is Mike taller than his younger brother John?
   I'm not sure. _____ boys are very tall.

9. Was there any food left over after the party last night?
   No. People were hungry. They ate _____.

10. Which presentation was the most interesting?
    I don't know. I think _____ student had something interesting to say.

B. Choose the best word to complete the sentence.

1. We have English class (all/every) Monday and Wednesday afternoon.
2. The guests ate (all/everything) the food on the table.
3. The students enjoyed (both/every) movies very much.
4. (Every/All) guest thanked the hostess after the party.
5. (Everyone/Everything) left the party at the same time.
6. That student missed (all/every) class last week.
7. We have to pass (every/both) courses to get credits.
8. Someone cleaned (everything/all) up after the party.
9. It was very cold yesterday so we stayed inside (all/every) day.
10. (All/Everyone) must have a boarding pass and passport.

| tall | short | hungry | a presentation | to thank | hosts |

Listening and Speaking: Using Idioms

At the Shopping Mall

A. Choose the expression that means the same as the words in bold type in each sentence.

1. Excuse me. I'm **looking for** a blue sweater in a small size. Do you have one?
   a) trying to find
   b) seeing

2. What kind of sweater do you **have in mind**?
   a) are you carrying
   b) are you thinking about

3. I have to buy my aunt a birthday present, and I'm at a **total loss** on what to get.
   a) I lost the information
   b) I don't have any ideas

4. Let's go into the department store and **look around**. Maybe we can find something on sale.
   a) look at many things
   b) turn in a circle

5. Why don't you try the store **next door**?
   a) that is beside this one
   b) that has the same door

6. I love this jacket but I **can't afford it**. It's really expensive.
   a) don't like it
   b) don't have enough money for it

7. **Hold on** a minute. There's someone at my door.
   a) hold my watch
   b) wait a short while

8. This job is **too good to be true**. I am very happy to have it.
   a) not real
   b) wonderful

9. These coats are all on sale. If you want to buy one, **take your pick**.
   a) pick it up
   b) choose the one you want

to clean up   to look for   a sweater   a jacket   a coat   a mall

B. Listen and answer the questions.

1. What does Tina want to buy?
2. What is the problem with the first store?
3. What is on sale at the store?
4. What does Tina think about the sweaters?

Turn to page 151 for Exercise C.

Ten-Minute Grammar Games

Bumping Words

Focus: Practise past participles.

Each box contains four words. Three of the words are similar. The word that is different should be "bumped" out to the next box. The next box will also contain three similar words, and one word that does not fit.

Students continue bumping the words until they reach the end. The last box contains one word that does not fit. They use that word to complete the sentence at the bottom. The first box has been done as an example.

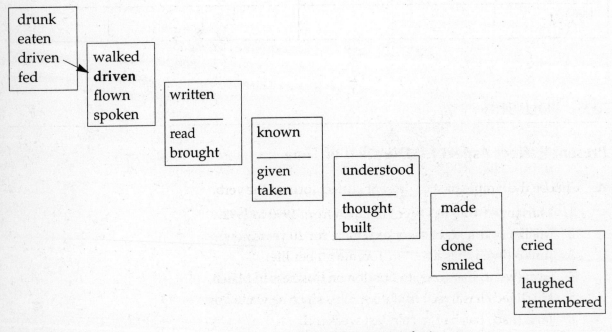

Good for you! You have _____ all the past participles!

Last Session

Focus: Puzzle.

Students solve the following problem by reading the clues and completing the chart.

Five students studied at the Wonderful Language Institute last session. They all studied in different classrooms and they all had different teachers. Which students studied in which classrooms and with which teachers?

1. Gaby was in Room 207.
2. Mr. Robb's class was on the second floor.
3. Ray and Tanya had class on the first floor.
4. Mrs. Jones was not Ray's teacher.
5. Sophie was Ms. Koop's student.
6. Sophie was in Room 203.
7. Mr. Grant's class was in Room 102.
8. The student in the class between Gaby and Sophie had a teacher named Miss Shaw.
9. Annie's class was on the second floor.

Room	#102	#104	#203	#206	#207
Student					
Teacher					

Test Yourself

Present Perfect Aspect for Duration of Time

A. Choose the simple past or present perfect form of the verb.

1. Marianne (was/has been) in Japan from 1990 to 1992.
2. Michel (worked/has worked) there for 10 years now.
3. Junko (lived/has lived) in Toronto all her life.
4. Sam (went/has gone) to London on business in March.
5. He (lived/has lived) next door to us since he was a boy.
6. Jane (had/has had) a cold last weekend.
7. I (knew/have known) those people since 1986.
8. Maria (worked/has worked) in Jakarta in 1987.
9. Jack (spoke/has spoken) Turkish when I met him.
10. Ali (was/has been) a student here since last September.

B. How will the receptionist answer the doctor's questions? Use the information in brackets and answer the doctor's questions with complete sentences. Use contractions.

1. How long has Mary been sick? (3 days)
2. How long has Anna been in the waiting room? (20 minutes)
3. How long has Pierre had a sore throat? (2 days)
4. How long have the children been home from school? (all week)
5. How long has Nadia had this fever? (24 hours)
6. How long has Giovanna been off work? (5 days)
7. How many headaches has she had this week? (3)
8. How long have they been married? (6 months)
9. How long has David had a cough? (6 days)
10. How long has Miguel had a sore neck? (2 days)

C. Use a sheet of paper. Change the sentences. Use **for** instead of **since**. Answer according to the time, day, and date it is now.

I have lived here since 1990. I have lived here for _____ years.

1. It has been cold since Tuesday.
2. We have been here since eight o'clock this morning.
3. Joe has worked here since March.
4. Paul has spoken English since I met him six months ago.
5. Sue and Bob have known each other since May 1994.
6. Keiko has had a cold since last Wednesday.
7. My brother has been at university since 1993.
8. They have lived next door to us since 1986.
9. I have spoken English since the class began.
10. Mike has worked in China since 1992.

"Everyone," "Everything," "All," "Every," "Both"

Complete the sentences with **everyone, everything, all, every,** or **both**.

1. We wanted to invite _____ to come to the party.
2. _____ person in the room was talking to someone.
3. My family _____ play musical instruments.
4. Pam and Tina felt sick. _____ ladies left early.
5. _____ the guests enjoyed the party very much.
6. At dinner _____ seat at the table was taken.
7. Tom likes cookies and cake. He tried _____ desserts after dinner.
8. The band played _____ my favourite songs.
9. _____ the food was prepared the day before the party.
10. The guests thanked the hostess for _____.

Idioms

Use an idiomatic expression to replace the boldface words in each sentence. Use the correct form of expressions below to help you.

to look for	to afford something
to have in mind	hold on/hold it
to be at a total loss	too good to be true
to look around	next door
to take your pick	

1. These school bags are very nice, and they are not expensive. You can **choose the one you like**.

2. My car is getting old, but I **don't have enough money** to buy a new one. I'll have to **try to find** something second-hand.

3. Everything is on sale at the department store. Let's go down tomorrow and **look at things**.

4. I need some new clothes. I'm going to the shopping mall to **try to find** something new.

5. Tomorrow is Jim's birthday. Some of his friends want to give him a gift, but I don't know what **ideas they have**.

6. My friend asked me to think of some ideas for her school project, but I **have no ideas at all**.

7. Does Roger live **in the house beside yours**? I often see you at the bus stop together.

8. I've always wanted a jacket like this, and my friends gave me exactly the one I've always wanted for my birthday. It's **wonderful**.

9. **Wait** a minute. I'm not ready to leave yet. I have to put on my coat.

Score for Test Yourself: _____
                                    50

Listening and Speaking: Using Idioms

At the Shopping Mall

C. Listen and write the missing words.

Tina: I'm looking _____ a birthday present for a friend of mine. Do you have any ideas, Karen?

Karen: I don't know. What did you have in _____, Tina?

Tina: I'm not sure. I've known Julie for years, but I'm still at a total _____ when it comes to buying her a gift.

Karen: Well, let's go into this store and look _____. Wow! Everything is really overpriced here. Maybe we should try the store next _____. I think they're having a sale.

Tina: That's okay by me. I don't think I can _____ anything here.

Karen: Hold _____ a minute. Did you see these beautiful sweaters? They're actually on sale—half price!

Tina: Boy, we nearly missed those. These prices are too _____ to be true. I'm sure Julie would love one of these sweaters. And with these prices and this selection, I can take my _____.

D. Practise the conversation with a partner.

E. Work with a partner. Write a new dialogue about shopping for a present. Use as many idioms as you can.

12

Present Perfect Aspect (2)
Indefinite Past Time
Intensifiers ("Very," "Too")

Past Participles

Base form	Past tense	Past participle
become	became	**become**
begin	began	**begun**
blow	blew	**blown**
come	came	**come**
drink	drank	**drunk**
eat	ate	**eaten**
drive	drove	**driven**
give	gave	**given**
go	went	**gone**
grow	grew	**grown**
know	knew	**known**
run	ran	**run**
see	saw	**seen**
sing	sang	**sung**
speak	spoke	**spoken**
take	took	**taken**
wear	wore	**worn**
write	wrote	**written**

Word Power

Work with a partner. Describe the activities you see in the pictures.

Understanding Grammar

UNDERSTAND: **Present Perfect Aspect for Indefinite Past Time**

Use the present perfect when the time that an action took place is not known or is not important. Use the present perfect for actions that were repeated at an **indefinite** time in the past.

> He has taken courses in English and math.
>
> I have seen that movie three times.

Use the present form (**has, have**) of the auxiliary verb. Use the past participle of the main verb.

Many verbs use the past tense (regular and irregular) form of the verb as the past participle:

> I have walked.   I have grown.

Other verbs use an irregular form for the past participle.

> I have made a mistake.

Some common irregular forms of the past participle are listed below. For a complete list see Appendix 2, page 211.

Base form	Past tense	Past participle
become	became	**become**
begin	began	**begun**
blow	blew	**blown**
come	came	**come**
drink	drank	**drunk**
eat	ate	**eaten**
drive	drove	**driven**
give	gave	**given**
go	went	**gone**
grow	grew	**grown**
know	knew	**known**
run	ran	**run**
see	saw	**seen**
sing	sang	**sung**
speak	spoke	**spoken**
take	took	**taken**
wear	wore	**worn**
write	wrote	**written**

Language in Transition

In some contexts, native speakers of English may replace the present perfect with the simple past when referring to indefinite past time. This is especially true in informal usage today: **I visited Florida many times.**

| to blow | to grow | to sing | to shop | hockey | soccer |

A. Choose the correct verb and put it in the present perfect form.

give   make   be   see   leave   write   take   drive   sing   go

1. John _____ that movie several times.
2. My brother and his wife _____ for China and Japan.
3. Janet _____ long letters to all her friends.
4. Hiroshi _____ some great pictures of New York.
5. My dad _____ several trips to Asia.
6. Tanya and Ray _____ both trucks and jeeps.
7. Max _____ to three different schools.
8. Maria and I _____ some great songs together.
9. My parents _____ on vacation for three weeks.
10. Julia _____ her sister a lot of help.

B. Choose the simple past or the present perfect form of the verb.

1. Sam (took/has taken) some good pictures with his new camera last week.
2. Jun and Lily (visited/have visited) Australia last year.
3. Marc (wore/has worn) his new jacket to the party.
4. Tanya (learned/has learned) to drive in high school.
5. My uncle (drank/has drunk) three cups of tea already.
6. We (spoke/have spoken) Spanish at the party last night.
7. I (wrote/have written) two letters home this month without an answer.
8. Maria (ate/has eaten) at my house many times.
9. Pierre (began/has begun) to speak English well.
10. Yoko (knew/has known) my sister when she lived in Kyoto.

UNDERSTAND: **"Already," "Just," and "Yet" with the Present Perfect**

Use **already** with the present perfect to refer to actions in the recent past. **Already** refers to actions that occurred **sooner than expected**. Put **already** between the auxiliary verb and the main verb.

We have **already** eaten.

a truck   a jeep   to visit   tea   a cup   to drink

Use **just** to refer to actions completed immediately before the moment when you are speaking. Put **just** between the auxiliary verb and the main verb.

They have **just** left.

Use **yet** to refer to actions that haven't happened but will probably happen in the future. Use **yet** in negative sentences and questions. Put **yet** at the end of the sentence.

It hasn't rained **yet**.

Has the package arrived **yet**?

A. Complete the conversations with **already, just,** or **yet**.

1. Are Miguel and Maria still here?
   You are one minute too late. They have _____ left.

2. Can I help you with anything?
   No thanks. Everything is _____ done.

3. Shall I call and cancel the appointment?
   It's okay. I've _____ cancelled it.

4. Is Caroline here?
   No, she hasn't arrived _____.

5. Will you write the exam this Thursday?
   No, I haven't studied for it _____.

6. Why do those people look so lost?
   Because they've _____ arrived in town.

7. Do you think we should buy a scarf for Susan?
   No, I think she has _____ got one.

8. Why is the sidewalk wet?
   Because it has _____ rained.

9. Are you going to write the exam on Thursday?
   No, I have _____ passed it.

10. Can we have dessert now?
    No, you haven't finished your main course _____.

a package   to cancel   lost   a scarf   a sidewalk   dessert

158

B. Look at the picture of Lili's birthday party with her friends and answer the questions. Use the present perfect form with **already** and **yet**. Use complete sentences.

| a birthday cake | candles | presents | film | to load | to finish |

1. Have they finished dinner?
2. Have they eaten the fish?
3. Have they served coffee?
4. Has Lili blown out the candles?
5. Has Lili cut the birthday cake?

6. Have they hung up the balloons?
7. Have they washed the dishes?
8. Has Lili opened her presents?
9. Have they sung Happy Birthday?
10. Have they taken a picture?

UNDERSTAND: **Present Perfect for Indefinite Past Time Negative**

The **negative** of the present perfect refers to actions or events that have **not** happened at the time you are speaking.

> I have been to Malaysia but **I haven't been** to Australia yet.

Use **never** with the present perfect to refer to an action that has not happened at any time.

> **He has never given** a speech in public. (not at any time)

Note: Do not use **never** with a negative verb. Double negatives are not permitted in English.

✔ I **have never** eaten sushi.

✘ I **haven't never** eaten sushi.

A. Choose the correct verb to complete the sentences. Use the negative form of the present perfect. Use contractions.

arrive   take   see   do   go   drink   eat   speak   begin   meet

1. Joyce and Paul _____ to each other for years.
2. We _____ anything to deserve such bad service.
3. The photographer _____ any pictures yet.
4. Leila _____ the tea she ordered with her dinner.
5. Alex _____ any of his vegetables yet.
6. They _____ to talk about the real problems yet.
7. My parents _____ to a movie for ages.
8. Jane and Sam _____ each other before.
9. William _____ the new movie yet.
10. Min is waiting at the station for her friend who _____ yet.

to serve

to cut

to open

sushi

a photographer

a station

B. Read the story. Then choose the statements that are **probably true** about Luc Roberge.

Luc Roberge is a dairy farmer in Quebec in Canada. He has lived on the farm all his life and he likes the quiet life in the country. He doesn't like the city and he doesn't like to be far from the farm. Luc loves nature. In the summer he takes his children camping or canoeing. In the winter he likes to cross-country ski in his spare time. When the snow is deep in the winter, Luc uses a snowmobile for transportation. When he retires, he and his wife plan to make their first trip to another country. They will visit France.

1. Luc has never had children.
2. He has never visited a foreign country.
3. His children have never gone camping.
4. He and his wife have never taken a plane.
5. Luc Roberge has never seen snow.
6. He has never made plans for the future.
7. He has never worn any kind of skis.
8. He has never been to Las Vegas for the weekend.
9. Luc and his wife have never visited France.
10. He has never stayed home because of deep snow.

UNDERSTAND: **Present Perfect For Indefinite Past Time Questions**

Use the present perfect for questions when you don't want to focus on when an action occurred. Use the simple past when the time an action occurred is mentioned. Look at the examples.

Have you ever been to Cairo? (at any time in your life)

Did you see the pyramids when you were in Egypt? (time is mentioned)

"Ever"

Ever (at any time) is often used with questions about indefinite past time. **Ever** follows the auxiliary verb and goes before the main verb.

Have you **ever** eaten oysters? (at any time)

A. Complete the chart for yourself. Then interview other students to see if they have ever done the following activities. Ask the question, "Have you ever...?"

country   city   a diary farm   a canoe   deep   shallow

	Me	Student A	Student B	Student C
Eaten oysters				
Spoken in public				
Smoked a cigar				
Seen an eclipse				
Met a famous person				
Ridden a horse				
Grown your hair long				
Sung in public				
Written a fan letter				
Made a birthday cake				
Been afraid of anything				
Gone on a trip alone				
Driven a truck				
Come to class late				
Taken a Spanish course				

B. Work in groups. Use a sheet of paper. Compare information with your group and make a list of three people who have:

never ridden a horse   met a famous person
written a fan letter   never made a birthday cake
never been afraid of anything   sung in public
never grown their hair long   taken a Spanish class
gone on a trip alone   eaten oysters
driven a truck   spoken in public
never come to class late   smoked a cigar
seen an eclipse

a snowmobile   oysters   a cigar   an eclipse   a horse   a fan letter

"Yet"

Use **yet** at the end of the sentence to ask about an action you think will occur in the near future.

Has she taken the picture yet?

Match the questions and the answers.

1. Has Maggie had lunch yet?
2. Has Junko been to New York yet?
3. Have you finished university yet?
4. Have you written to your sister yet?
5. Has Paul studied for the exam yet?
6. Have you got a passport yet?
7. Have they eaten dinner yet?
8. Has the rain stopped yet?
9. Has Marc's bus left yet?
10. Have you been to the store yet?

a) No, it hasn't stopped yet.
b) Yes, I have already graduated.
c) Yes, she has already eaten.
d) No, they haven't eaten yet.
e) Yes, it left ten minutes ago.
f) Yes, she has already had two letters.
g) No, I haven't got one yet.
h) Yes, she has already been there.
i) No, he hasn't studied yet.
j) No, I haven't been yet.

UNDERSTAND: **Intensifiers ("Very," "Too")**

Use **very** as an adverb of degree. Put **very** before the adjective.

Use **too** to give the idea of more than necessary. Put **too** before the adjective or adverb. Put **too** before **much, many, few,** and **little.**

heavy   light   a piano   to graduate   lunch   a passport

A. Complete the sentence with **very** or **too**.

1. I can't eat that piece of cake. It's _____ big.
2. Your dress is pretty. You look _____ beautiful.
3. Nancy has a _____ busy day at work tomorrow.
4. They cancelled the play. There were _____ few people.
5. I'm thirsty. I'd like a glass of _____ cold water.
6. They are planning a _____ big party on Saturday.
7. Janet couldn't wear my jacket because it was _____ small.
8. Jim called. He is _____ busy to meet us for lunch.
9. Miko has a big appetite. He often eats _____ much.
10. We didn't get tickets. The price was _____ high.

B. Some sentences have errors. Find the errors and correct them.

1. Keiko is a good pianist. She plays too well.
2. After work Maria is sometimes very tired to cook.
3. Miguel makes mistakes if he works too quickly.
4. Brazil has a good climate but it is very hot.
5. He arrived too late but he caught the train anyway.
6. Max got to the bus stop too late and missed the bus.
7. John was very sick to go to work on Wednesday.
8. The temperature was very cold to stay outside long.
9. Ask Lisa to help move the piano. She is too strong.
10. Mei made an excellent dinner. She cooks very well.

Listening and Speaking: Using Idioms

Moving In

A. Find the meaning for the words in bold type.

1. **So far** I've only finished half my homework. I'd better hurry up.
   a) until now   b) a long distance

2. This room is a big mess. You'd better **put away** your books and clothes before your mother comes home.
   a) throw out   b) put in the proper places

a mistake   curtains   a coin   a surgeon   to get rid of   a sofa

3. These clothes are old and torn. I'm going to **get rid of them**.
   a) throw them out   b) use them

4. My uncle is overweight and he smokes too much. He's really in **bad shape**.
   a) bad condition   b) big size

5. My sister's house needs a lot of repairs. She doesn't have enough money to buy a new house, so she'll have to **fix up** the one she has.
   a) get others   b) repair

6. Your boss needs this report right away. You'd better do it **at once**.
   a) one time   b) immediately

7. I've had these shoes for five years. They have holes in the soles. I guess you can say they are **worn out**.
   a) too old to wear   b) worn outside

8. I'd like to travel this summer, but it's **out of the question**. I just don't have enough money.
   a) something to ask about   b) impossible

9. This apartment is a little small for now, but we can't afford anything else, so we'll have to **make the best of it**.
   a) do what we can   b) make something good

B. Listen and answer the questions.

1. When did Margaret move into her apartment?
2. What has Margaret bought so far?
3. When will she shop for new things?
4. Why did she have to get rid of most of her furniture?
5. What is the problem with Margaret's sofa?
6. Why can't she buy a new one?
7. What does Rita plan to do until she has more money?

Turn to page 168 for Exercise C.

Ten-Minute Grammar Games

Puzzles

Focus: Puzzle.

Students work with a partner to solve these puzzles.

1. A surgeon looked at the young patient who was brought to the emergency room by ambulance and turned pale. The doctor gasped, "I can't operate on my son." The nurse replied, "I'll get another surgeon right away." Then she hurried out to call the boy's father who was at work and didn't know the boy was injured. Who was the surgeon?

2. A person had two coins with a value of 30 cents, but one of the coins was not a quarter (25 cents). What two coins did the person have?

Participles

Focus: Practise past participles.

Students write the past participle of each verb. Then they discover the hidden words.

1. pay
2. run
3. eat
4. see
5. go
6. sing
7. take
8. put
9. give
10. drink
11. feel
12. become
13. come
14. write

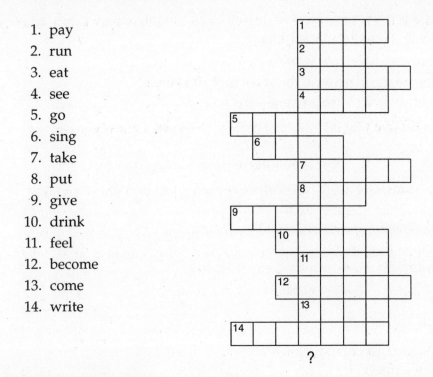

?

The Old and the New

Focus: Practise present perfect with **yet**.

Look at the pictures. The house on the left has been bought by the Simpson family. They are in the process of renovating it.

Write sentences about what has been changed in the house, and what hasn't been done yet.

The front door has been changed.

New flowers haven't been planted yet.

Test Yourself

Present Perfect Aspect for Indefinite Past Time

A. Complete the sentences using the simple past or the present perfect.

1. Annabel _____ (learn) three languages.
2. Jackson _____ (drive) to work yesterday.
3. My family _____ (visited) Greece in 1994.
4. Hiroki _____ (eat) Mexican food several times.
5. Jeannot _____ (worked) in a store last summer.
6. Pedro _____ (go) to Malaysia several times.
7. Suzy and Tanya _____ (be) to hockey games before.
8. Jenna and I _____ (make) dinner yesterday.
9. Barbara and Tom _____ (fall) in love.
10. I _____ (speak) to him about it twice already.

B. Some sentences have errors. Find the errors and correct them.

1. Have you ever been to the Olympic stadium?
2. We haven't never gone to Florida.
3. Keiko and Carla haven't never met before.
4. Has anyone here never eaten raw oysters?
5. Have you ever ridden on the back of a motorcycle?
6. Michael has never tried downhill skiing.
7. Carolyn hasn't never studied another language.
8. Junko hasn't never been afraid of anything.
9. Has the Eiffel Tower ever been painted?
10. Gaby hasn't never been sick in her life.

C. Complete the conversation by putting **ever**, **never**, **already**, or **yet** in the correct place in the sentences.

Ben: This is a wonderful hotel. Have you _____ stayed here before?

Jerry: No, _____, but Ellen has stayed here a few times. She has _____ booked it for her next trip.

Ben: I hear they have a great swimming pool. Have you tried the swimming pool _____?

Jerry: No, not _____. I want to eat something first. Do you want to join me?

Ben: Sure. I know a good restaurant. Have you _____ eaten Japanese food? This place has great sushi.

Jerry: I've eaten Japanese food, but I've _____ eaten sushi.

Ben: I've _____ made reservations for seven o'clock. It isn't seven o'clock _____.

Jerry: We haven't tried the pool _____. Let's take a swim and then go for dinner.

Ben: Great idea. Then when we arrive at the restaurant, we'll _____ have a good appetite.

Intensifiers

Complete the sentences with the intensifiers **very** or **too**.

1. We were _____ tired to go downtown this morning.
2. This jacket is _____ big for me. I need a smaller size.
3. Max can't eat everything. There is _____ much on his plate.
4. Celia won the competition. She played _____ well.
5. The weather in Canada is _____ cold in the winter.
6. We need a bigger room. There are _____ many people here.
7. Maybe my brother can help you. He is _____ good at math.
8. Rick got a new car. His old one needed _____ many repairs.
9. I think I'll wait. This coffee is _____ hot to drink now.
10. Someone stole Jack's watch. He is _____ angry about it.

Idioms

Complete the paragraphs using idioms. Use the correct form of these expressions to help you.

so far	at once
to put something away	to be worn out
to get rid of	out of the question
to be in bad shape	to make the best of something
to fix up	

Monica and Victor have just bought a house. The house is old, and it's in pretty bad _____, but Monica and Victor are not worried because they plan to _____ it up. They know that they can't do everything _____ once. That would be _____ of the question, since they don't have a lot of money right now. _____ far they have painted three rooms, and they have got _____ of some old wallpaper in the bathroom. The kitchen counter is old and _____ out too, but that is too expensive to repair, so they will have to make the _____ of it for a while.

For now, they will _____ away all their dishes and cutlery. Then they will begin to fix _____ the kitchen a little at a time.

Score for Test Yourself: _____

50

Listening and Speaking: Using Idioms

Moving In

C.   Listen and write the words.

Rita:	Hi Margaret. How's your new apartment?
Margaret:	Not bad, Rita. I just moved in a week ago, and I'm still unpacking boxes.
Rita:	Have you got a lot of new furniture yet?
Margaret:	Just a rug so _____. As soon as I put everything _____ I'll start looking for the new things I need.
Rita:	Didn't you have a lot of furniture in your old apartment?
Margaret:	I did, but I had to get rid _____ a lot of things. Most of my furniture was in pretty bad _____.
Rita:	Well, it will be nice when everything is fixed _____.
Margaret:	I know. I'm looking forward to that. The problem is that I can't afford to do everything at _____. My sofa is really worn _____, but buying a new one now is out of the _____.
Rita:	I know what you mean. I'd love to _____ up my apartment too, but I don't have much money right now. I guess I'll just have to make the _____ of it.

D.   Practise the dialogue with a partner.

E.   Work with a partner. Write a new dialogue about moving into an new apartment. Use as many idioms as you can.

13

Future Time

With the Auxiliary "Will"
With the Phrase "Be going to"
With the Present Tenses

"Will"

Affirmative		
I will		
you will		
he will		
she will		
it will	work	
we will		
you will		
they will		

Negative		
I will not		
you will not		
he will not		
she will not		
it will not	work	
we will not		
you will not		
they will not		

Question Form		
will I		
will you		
will he		
will she		
will it	work?	
will we		
will you		
will they		

"Be going to"

Affirmative		
I am going to		
you are going to		
he is going to		
she is going to		
it is going to	work	
we are going to		
you are going to		
they are going to		

Negative		
I am not going to		
you are not going to		
he is not going to		
she is not going to		
it is not going to	work	
we are not going to		
you are not going to		
they are not going to		

Word Power

Work with a partner. Describe what you see in the picture.

Understanding Grammar

UNDERSTAND: **Future Time**

English does not have a future tense. To refer to future time, use

1. the modal auxiliary **will**
2. the verb phrase **be going to**
3. the present tenses (simple or continuous)

UNDERSTAND: **"Will" for Future Time**

Use **will** + the base form of the main verb for:

1. offers or promises relating to the future—that is, to say what you are willing to do:

   Don't worry. I'll run out and make some photocopies.

2. predictions related to what we personally believe will happen in the future:

   I think the company will probably need more employees next year.

3. formal announcements of future events:

   There will be a meeting of all office staff at two o'clock tomorrow.

The contraction of will is 'll (**I'll go**.)

Affirmative			Contraction		
I will			I'll		
you will			you'll		
he will			he'll		
she will			she'll		
it will		work	it'll		work
we will			we'll		
you will			you'll		
they will			they'll		

Read the letter and respond to the statements with short answers. Use the form **Yes, she will** for affirmative answers, and **No, she won't** for negative answers.

Jane will be late for dinner. **Yes, she will.**

a computer   a typewriter   a fax machine   a photocopier   a secretary   a receptionist

Dear Tom,

I forgot to tell you that I will be late for dinner tonight. We have an important meeting at the office. The meeting probably won't begin on time so we won't be out of there before six o'clock.

I'll leave as soon as I can, but I'm sure that Sue will want a ride, so I'm not sure what time I will be home. Please call Mike and tell him that I'll drive Sue home on the way.

You'll find some cold chicken in the fridge. Put it in the oven at 350 degrees. It will be ready in 15 minutes. I'll be hungry when I get home so don't eat all the chicken!

Love Jane

1. There will be a meeting at Tom's office.
2. The meeting will begin on time.
3. The meeting will be over by five o'clock.
4. Jane will leave right after the meeting.
5. Sue will drive her car home after work.
6. Jane will be home at six o'clock.
7. Mike will drive Sue home.
8. The chicken will be ready in ten minutes.
9. Jane will be hungry when she gets home.
10. Jane will eat chicken for supper.

Negative Form

Use **will not** + the base form of the main verb for negation in future time. The contraction of **will not** is **won't**.

> Smoking **will not** be permitted in this office.
>
> I **won't** make that mistake again.
>
> We **won't** need to order more paper for a while.

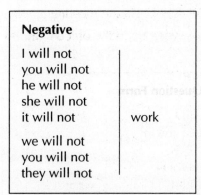

Negative

I will not	
you will not	
he will not	
she will not	
it will not	work
we will not	
you will not	
they will not	

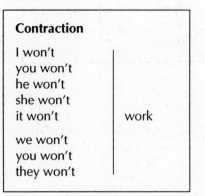

Contraction

I won't	
you won't	
he won't	
she won't	
it won't	work
we won't	
you won't	
they won't	

| chicken | an oven | a meeting | a desk | a stapler | a paper clip |

Write the negative form of these sentences. Use the contraction **won't**.

> She will get the job. She **won't** get the job.

1. The meeting will be in the boardroom today.
2. The meeting will be over by three o'clock.
3. It will be easy to get a dentist's appointment today.
4. John will tell us what happened at the meeting.
5. She will be out of the office all afternoon.
6. The new receptionist will remember to turn off the coffee maker.
7. The photocopies of the forms will be ready today.
8. The boss will interview all the applicants tomorrow.
9. The decision will be made this afternoon.
10. The office will be open at eight o'clock.

Question Form

Use **will** + the subject + the base form of the main verb to ask questions about future events.

> Will they begin the meeting at two o'clock?
>
> Will everyone in the office work on Thanksgiving?

Question Form	
will I	
will you	
will he	
will she	
will it	work?
will we	
will you	
will they	

Language in Transition

In the past, the affirmative for **will** in the first person was **shall**. Today, it is more common to say **I will**, **we will**. **Shall** is used in some formulaic questions that do the following:

1. **ask for advice:**
   What shall we buy next?
2. **make offers:**
   Shall I answer the door?
3. **make suggestions:**
   Shall we meet at six o'clock?

a boardroom   a coffee maker   a form   an application   a binder   a folder

A. Match the questions and answers.

What time will he be here? He'll be here at one o'clock.

1. When will the new secretary start?
2. How will you get to work tomorrow?
3. Who will replace Fred next week?
4. How long will the coffee break be?
5. When will she order more paper?
6. How will people find out about the job?
7. What will happen if he's late again?
8. Where will they put the photocopier?
9. How will we know what they need?
10. What time will you phone me?

a) He'll really be in trouble.
b) They'll ask Moira to fill in.
c) I'll call in the early afternoon.
d) They'll put it in the stockroom.
e) I think she'll start on Monday.
f) It'll be 15 minutes.
g) There'll be an ad in the paper.
h) I'll probably take a taxi.
i) They'll send us a fax.
j) She'll probably order some on Monday.

B. Fill in the blanks. Use **will** or **shall**. Use the formulaic **shall** for advice, offers, and suggestions.

1. You look tired. _____ I call a taxi for you?
2. We need more fax paper. Who _____ order it?
3. The secretary isn't here. Who _____ take the minutes?
4. The storage room is full. Where _____ they put the new supplies?
5. I'm hungry. Where _____ we go for lunch?
6. Excuse me, I need to make some photocopies. When _____ the machine be free?
7. We need this document translated. Who _____ we ask to do it?
8. I'm thirsty. When _____ the coffee be ready?
9. The meeting is over. _____ we go?
10. Miguel is in town. _____ I invite him to join us?

late   a coffee break   to order   a stockroom   supplies   an ad

UNDERSTAND: **"Be going to" for Future Time**

Use **be going to** + the base form of the main verb for:

1. predictions that result from present events:

   Everyone is here. I think the meeting **is going to start** any minute.

2. statement of intentions resulting from plans or decisions.

For your own plans or intentions you can use **be going to** or **will**:

   He is going to join us later.

   He will join us later.

For other people's plans or intentions you normally use **be going to**:

   They are going to put an ad in the paper.

Affirmative		Contraction	
I am going to		I'm going to	
you are going to		you're going to	
he is going to		he's going to	
she is going to	work	she's going to	work
it is going to		it's going to	
we are going to		we're going to	
you are going to		you're going to	
they are going to		they're going to	

A. Look at Lili's agenda. Use the information to answer the questions. Answer with complete sentences.

Lili's Agenda   **APRIL 1–7**

Sunday	Monday	Tuesday	Wednesday	Thursday	Friday	Saturday
Go to bed early	Taxi 8 am Meet Joseph 8:30, my office	Lunch: Anne Start report	Finish report (am) Work on budget (pm)	Ask Louise to copy report Meet Susan: boardroom	Sales meeting	

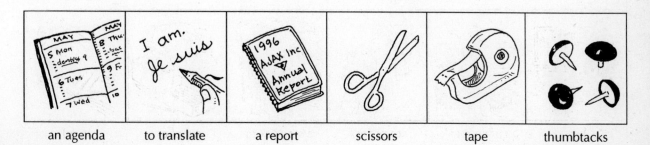

an agenda · to translate · a report · scissors · tape · thumbtacks

1. How is Lili going to get to work on Tuesday?
2. Which day is she going to go to bed early?
3. Who is she going to meet on Monday morning?
4. What time is the meeting going to start?
5. When is she going to finish the report?
6. Who is she going to ask to photocopy the report?
7. When is she going to meet Anne for lunch?
8. When is she going to attend the sales meeting?
9. What is she going to do on Wednesday afternoon?
10. Where is she going to meet Susan?

Language in Transition

When the main verb following **be going to** is **go**, it is possible to omit the main verb:
She is going to bed early tomorrow.

B. Match the problem and the solution. Then write out the solution using **be going to**.

Max needs a French translation.   ask Henri to do it

Max is going to ask Henri to do it.

1. Frank locked his keys in the office.
2. Maria can't fix the photocopier.
3. Kim wants a cup of coffee.
4. Anne's telephone is ringing.
5. Marco needs a report typed.
6. Henri and Jack need to smoke.
7. Irene is feeling really sick.
8. Tom has a plane to catch at four o'clock.
9. Yoko and Mei missed their bus.
10. Tan needs more invoice forms today.

a) answer it
b) go outside to smoke
c) leave the office early
d) go home and rest
e) take a taxi to work
f) call security
g) put in a rush order
h) call the repairman
i) get one from the coffee machine
j) ask his secretary to type it

a stapler   staples   a glue stick   to lock   keys   a calculator

Negative Form

Use **not** after the verb **be** and before **going to** for negation in future time:

> I am **not** going to study tonight.

The contraction is used in spoken English and informal written English. Either form of the contraction can be used with **be going to**:

> He's not going to come with us.

> He isn't going to come with us.

Negative	**Contraction A**	**Contraction B**
I am not going to you are not going to he is not going to she is not going to it is not going to work we are not going to you are not going to they are not going to	I'm not going to you're not going to he's not going to she's not going to it's not going to work we're not going to you're not going to they're not going to	 you aren't going to he isn't going to she isn't going to it isn't going to work we aren't going to you aren't going to they aren't going to

Some sentences have errors. Find the errors and correct them.

1. The repairman is not going to come and fix the photocopier today.
2. The security man no is going to be here soon.
3. Tan is not go to order new forms today.
4. Irene is not going go home early today.
5. Tom is not going to take a bus to the airport.
6. The photocopies are not going be ready in time.
7. Kim is not going to make coffee for everyone.
8. Maria is going call a repairman to fix the machine.
9. Henri is not go to smoke in the office.
10. Marco is no going to ask a secretary to type his report.

an adding machine   to fix   a rush order   a cordless phone   a receiver   a cord

Question Form

Use the verb **be** + the subject + **going to** + the base form of the main verb for the question form.

When is the meeting going to start?

Is the ad campaign going to begin in July?

Question	
am I going to	
are you going to	
is he going to	
is she going to	
is it going to	work?
are we going to	
are you going to	
are they going to	

Write questions about the plans for the meeting.

1. The sales meeting is going to be tomorrow.
   When _____?

2. Marco and Tom are going to arrange the chairs.
   What _____?

3. Anne is going to put flowers on the head table.
   Where _____?

4. Kim and Frank are going to distribute copies of the annual report.
   What _____?

5. Gino is going to empty the wastepaper baskets and clean the carpets.
   What _____?

6. Keiko is going to order the food and beverages for the break.
   Who _____?

7. The president is going to open the meeting by welcoming everyone.
   How _____?

8. Everyone is going to arrive at 9:00.
   When _____?

9. The meeting is going to finish at four o'clock.
   What time _____?

10. Jack and Steve are going to clean up after the meeting.
    When _____?

an ad campaign   a head table   to distribute   wastepaper basket   a carpet   beverages

UNDERSTAND: **Using the Present Simple or Present Continuous for Future Time**

In certain situations present tenses are used to talk about future events or activities.

1. Use the present simple to talk about **scheduled events** in the future.
   Jack's plane leaves in an hour. (It is scheduled to leave.)

2. Use the present continuous to talk about **future arrangements**.
   We are meeting at the airport. (It is an arrangement.)

TEACHER'S BOX: In the sentence, **We are meeting at the airport**, the focus is on the arrangement. The present continuous is used to focus on arrangements. However, in the sentence, **I am going to meet Anne at the bus stop**, the focus is on an intention. The **be + going to** form is used to focus on a future intention.

a microphone   a podium   a water pitcher   flowers   to welcome   to shake hands

180

Choose the correct form of the verb. If it is a scheduled event, use the present simple. If it is an arrangement, use the present continuous form.

1. Four people from our office _____ (go) to a convention in Boston next week.
2. The convention _____ (start) early Wednesday morning.
3. We _____ (fly) to Boston after work on Tuesday.
4. Our flight _____ (land) at 8:00 in the evening.
5. We _____ (stay) at the Omni Hotel near the Convention Centre.
6. Registration _____ (begin) at eight o'clock sharp.
7. We _____ (meet) in the coffee shop to have breakfast first.
8. The convention _____ (end) Friday afternoon.
9. We _____ (leave) for the airport at five o'clock.
10. Our plane _____ (take off) at 6:20.

Listening and Speaking: Using Idioms

A Meeting

A. Study the idioms in these sentences.

1. You are late this morning. You **had better** hurry, or you'll miss the bus.
2. Bob hasn't arrived at work yet. He usually **gets in** at 9:30.
3. The party is Friday night, but I can't **make it** because I already have plans.
4. Julie is home sick today, so we'll have to **carry on** without her.
5. I'll be late for the meeting tomorrow. Can you **fill me in** on the details when I arrive?
6. I don't understand the report that you wrote. Could you please **go over** it with me?
7. I hear that there's a party next week. Do you know where it will **take place**?
8. We'd better hurry. The show starts at 8:00 **on the dot**.

B. Match the expressions on the left to the meanings on the right. Use the sentences above to help you.

1. had better
2. to get in
3. to make it
4. to carry on

a) to occur, to happen
b) should
c) to give someone information
d) to arrive

to register   a coffee shop   a cafeteria   to empty   to beep   a courier

5. to fill someone in   e) at the exact time
6. to go over   f) to get there
7. to take place   g) to continue
8. on the dot   h) to review, to check

C. Listen and answer the questions.

1. Why does Kim think she should go to the meeting?
2. What time does Terry's plane get in?
3. How will Terry get the information he needs?
4. What time does the meeting start?

Turn to page 185 for Exercise D.

Ten-Minute Grammar Games

Destinations

Focus: Practise future with **going to** and **will**.

Students choose five objects from the list below, and write a short paragraph about what will happen to each. They should be as imaginative as they can:

> The pen is going to be used by a traveller. The traveller will put the pen in his pocket to use on the airplane. The pen will travel all over the world, and be used to write great news stories.

a pencil   a piece of chocolate   a pair of scissors   a $10 bill   a car tire

a paper bag   a bar of soap   a comb   a hammer and nails   some fabric

a stapler   a cup of coffee   a brick   a bird   a chair

Future Predictions

Focus: Practise future with **going to** and **will**.

The teacher writes the name of each student in the class on a piece of paper, and puts the names in a bag. Students each pull out one paper.

Students write future predictions for the student whose name they have. They write **only good things**, but they should be as detailed and imaginative as they can.

Students take turns reading their predictions to the class.

Solve the Problem

Focus: Practise future with **going to** and **will**.

Students solve the following problem by reading the clues and completing the chart.

Ambassadors from four countries have just been posted to new cities. They have to be in the new cities on certain dates. They will travel by different airlines. Which ambassadors are going where, when, and on which airline?

1. The Mexican ambassador is going to Istanbul.
2. The ambassador who will fly on February 25 is from Egypt.
3. The flight on May 21 is Singapore Air.
4. The ambassador who is going to Paris will fly on Air France.
5. The ambassador who flies on January 22 will fly JAL.
6. The Russian ambassador is not going to Ottawa.
7. The Chinese ambassador is going to Tokyo.
8. The flight on December 26 is Air France, not Swiss Air.
9. The ambassador who will fly to Istanbul will go on January 22.

Ambassador from:	Mexico	Russia	Egypt	China
Airline				
Date				
City				

Test Yourself

Future with "Will"

A. Choose the correct verbs. Put them in the future with **will**.

beep   phone   take   empty   get   leave   join   ask   meet   tell

1. I think the last candidate _____ the job.
2. The salesman _____ before he comes by.
3. Martin _____ us for lunch tomorrow.
4. The receptionist _____ the visitors to wait.
5. Marla _____ a taxi to work on Friday.
6. The courier _____ the package at the front desk.
7. Joseph _____ you at the front door of the building.
8. The janitor _____ the wastepaper baskets for us.
9. The telephone _____ when there is another call on the line.
10. Kevin _____ us when the coffee is ready.

B. Complete the sentences with **will** or **won't**.

1. Andre really doesn't look very well. I'm sure he _____ be in tomorrow.
2. We need to replace the fax machine. How much do you think it _____ cost?
3. The demonstration is scheduled for three o'clock. What time do you think it _____ start?
4. The office staff is all new. You probably _____ recognize anybody.
5. Janet is quite shy. She probably _____ say much at the meeting tomorrow.
6. Kim invited the new employees to the meeting. Do you think they _____ all come?
7. They were very angry yesterday. How do you think they _____ feel tomorrow?
8. Don't worry about such a small mistake. Anyway, I'm sure it _____ happen again.
9. Lili and Chen have a long vacation this year. Where do you think they _____ go?
10. The repairman from the company fixed the photocopier. We _____ have to buy a new one.

Future with "Be going to"

Find the errors. Correct any verb phrases that are wrong.

They are going work together tomorrow.   are going **to**

1. I am no going to come to work tomorrow morning.
2. The meeting are going to end at seven o'clock.
3. Roberto is going work at home this afternoon.
4. We is not going to meet in the boardroom today.
5. She is going to buys stamps at the post office.
6. Tom is not going to get a raise in pay this month.
7. Lily and Carla are going take the bus to work tomorrow.
8. Roberto's report is not going be ready on time.
9. We are all going get together after work.
10. I think it is going to rain. Do you have an umbrella?

Future Using Present Tenses

Write questions using the present simple or present continuous form of the verbs.

1. Dan's plane gets in sometime in the afternoon.
   When _____?

2. The monthly meeting takes place in the boardroom.
   Where _____?

3. Sylvia is leaving early on Tuesday. She has a dentist's appointment
   Why _____?

4. The repairman is coming sometime this morning.
   When _____?

5. The switchboard opens at nine o'clock Monday.
   What time _____?

6. Dan is meeting his boss in the restaurant.
   Where _____?

7. He is bringing his luggage with him to the office.
   What _____?

8. Janice is taking her holidays in August this year.
   When _____?

9. She leaves for Paris and Barcelona on August 3rd.
   When _____?

10. Susan is replacing her in the office when she leaves.
    Who _____?

Idioms

Use an idiomatic expression to replace the words in bold type in each sentence. Use the correct form of these expressions to help you.

had better	to get in
to make it	to carry on
to fill someone in	to go over something
to take place	on the dot

1. The meeting starts at 7:00 **exactly**. Don't be late.
2. The meeting **will be** in my office, but the party afterwards will be in the room next door.
3. What time **do you arrive** tomorrow? I'd like to meet as soon as possible.
4. If I'm late tomorrow, I hope someone can **give me the information that I need**.
5. I don't understand the homework today. Maybe we can **review it** together later.
6. Some people are late today because of the bad weather, but we'll have to **continue** until they **arrive**.

7. A few of us are getting together tomorrow night. Do you think you can **be there**?

8. I think we **should** review the plans once more before we leave for the airport.

9. I hear that something interesting happened at the meeting yesterday, but I don't know the details. Can you **tell me what happened**?

Score for Test Yourself: _____
50

Listening and Speaking: Using Idioms

A Meeting

D. Listen and write the words.

Alberto: Are you going to the meeting this afternoon, Kim?

Kim: Yeah, I think I'd _____, Alberto. We have a lot to discuss. By the way, will Terry be at the meeting?

Alberto: I don't think so. His plane gets _____ at 3:00. I don't think he'll make _____ on time.

Kim: Oh well, we'll have to carry _____ without him. Someone will have to fill him _____ later.

Alberto: No problem. I can go _____ the information with him tomorrow.

Kim: Where will the meeting take _____?

Alberto: In the board room. It starts at 2:00 on the _____.

Kim: Okay. See you there.

E. Practise the conversation with a partner.

F. Write a new dialogue about a meeting. Use as many idioms as you can.

Conditional Sentences (Type 1)
Indefinite Pronouns

Indefinite Pronouns

everyone	someone	anyone	no one
everybody	somebody	anybody	nobody
everything	something	anything	nothing
everywhere	somewhere	anywhere	nowhere

Word Power

Work with a partner to describe what you see.

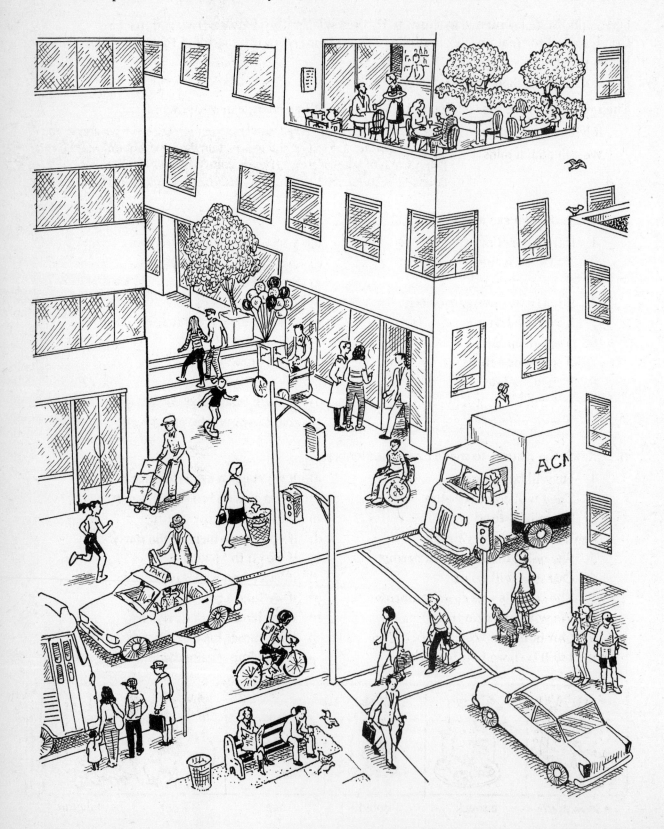

Understanding Grammar

UNDERSTAND: **Conditional Sentences (Type I)**

Use a conditional sentence to show an **if/then** relationship between two actions. Use Conditional I for real future possibility. The **if** clause gives the condition that will make a future action possible:

> **If** X happens, **then** Y will happen.

The **if** clause can be first or last in the sentence with no change in meaning:

> **If** it rains, we will go.
> We will go **if** it rains.

> **TEACHER'S BOX:** Conditional II (present unreal) and Conditional III (past unreal) appear in *Grammar Connections 3*.

A. Match the clauses to make logical sentences.

1. If it snows tonight,	a) you will play well.
2. If the bus is late,	b) you can have a snack.
3. If we study hard,	c) we will feel rested.
4. If we have enough players,	d) they will phone.
5. If you are hungry,	e) we will have good marks.
6. If we sleep late,	f) we will take it.
7. If the phone rings,	g) I will answer it.
8. If they are late,	h) we will have a team.
9. If the ticket is still available,	i) we will take a taxi.
10. If you practise enough,	j) the streets will be dangerous.

B. Match the clauses to make logical sentences.

1. He will be hungry	a) if we stay up until midnight.
2. They will come for sure	b) if she gets an increase in salary.
3. We will be tired	c) if there is a snow storm.
4. It will snow later today	d) if you invite them to the party.
5. She will probably work harder	e) if we go to Mexico.
6. Our rent will go up	f) if I stay home all day.
7. The schools will close tomorrow	g) if we take a taxi.
8. We will arrive on time	h) if the landlord does repairs.
9. Our holidays will be a lot of fun	i) if he misses his lunch break.
10. I will be bored on Saturday	j) if the temperature continues to go down.

a snowstorm   a snack   bored   rent   tenant   landlord

The **if** clause describes a condition that is necessary for something to happen. Use present time for the **if** clause. The main clause describes what will happen in future. Use future time for the main clause.

If it rains, we will take an umbrella.

present   future

> **TEACHER'S BOX:** Present time can be present simple, present continuous, or a modal verb phrase. However, it is preferable to introduce the concept of Conditional I sentences with the simple tense to avoid confusion.

C. Put the verbs in the correct tense.

1. If the phone in the office _____ (ring), the receptionist _____ (answer) it.

2. We _____ (call) a repairman from the company if the photocopier _____ (break) down.

3. Janet _____ (arrive) at work late if there _____ (be) a snow storm.

4. If someone _____ (be) sick, other employees _____ (do) that person's work.

5. If an employee always _____ (come) to work late, he or she _____ (get) fired.

6. This company _____ (hire) a lot of new people if the economy _____ (improve).

7. The secretary over there _____ (order) more paper, if you _____ (ask) her.

8. If there _____ (be) an opening, the company _____ (put) an ad in the paper.

9. Everyone _____ (be) happy if we _____ (hear) that there is a raise in salary.

10. If I _____ (collect) the money for coffee, we _____ (save) time at the breaks.

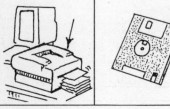   

a printer   a disk   a pencil sharpener   a paper cutter   a file cabinet   a rolodex

D. Some sentences have errors. Find the errors and correct them.

1. If you will make a good impression, you will get the job.
2. Henri will cook dinner tonight if we will be lucky.
3. If the exam will be today, we will all fail.
4. If he gets up too late, he will miss the school bus.
5. They will watch the news if they will get home in time.
6. The fans will be disappointed if they will cancel the game.
7. If the cat is hungry, it will meow for food.
8. If we will go to the party, we have a good time.
9. If Gaston asks Fifi to dance, she will accept.
10. The teacher will know if we will cheat on the exam.

UNDERSTAND: **Negation with Conditional I Sentences**

One or both clauses in a conditional sentence can be negative. The **if** clause is in present time and the main clause is in future time. The negative form of **will** is **won't (will not)**. Look at the examples of conditional sentences using negatives.

If it rains, we won't go.

If it doesn't rain, we will go.

If it isn't sunny, we won't go.

A. Put the verb of the main clause in the negative form.

1. If it rains, we will go to the picnic.
2. If the pay is low, I will accept that job.
3. The team will win if their best player is injured.
4. My brother will change jobs if he gets a raise in pay.
5. I will be late for work if I leave immediately.
6. If they rent two movies, they will go to bed early.
7. If he is really tired, he will stay up late.
8. If her suitcase is heavy, she will carry it herself.
9. The elevator will work well if it is overloaded.
10. The car will start easily if it is –32 degrees.

| a clipboard | to cheat | to meow | a picnic | to overload | injured |

B. Choose correct endings for these sentences.

1. If you come to an interview late,
   a) you'll get the job.
   b) you won't get the job.

2. If you make a good impression,
   a) they won't hire you.
   b) they'll hire you.

3. If you don't watch out,
   a) you'll get hurt.
   b) you won't get hurt.

4. If he smokes cigarettes,
   a) he won't stay healthy.
   b) he'll stay healthy.

5. If they don't practise,
   a) they will win the game.
   b) they won't win the game.

6. If they don't hurry up,
   a) they won't be on time.
   b) they'll be on time

7. If he doesn't stop smoking,
   a) it will affect his health.
   b) it won't affect his health.

8. If I don't wash the dishes,
   a) my mother will be happy.
   b) my mother won't be happy.

9. If the temperature goes down,
   a) we'll need coats.
   b) we won't need coats.

10. If we are late for dinner,
    a) they won't be angry.
    b) they'll be angry.

UNDERSTAND: **Questions with Conditional I**

The main clause can be a question about the future. The **if** clause is always in present time.

Will they cancel the picnic if it rains?

If we are late, **will they let** us in?

A. Match the two parts of the sentence.

1. What will we wear
2. Will the teacher be angry
3. If it snows tomorrow,
4. If we speak English,
5. How will we pass the exam
6. Will they go to the beach
7. If it doesn't rain,
8. If I exercise every day,
9. If the phone rings,
10. What will they do

a) if we don't study?
b) will people understand us?
c) if it's sunny tomorrow?
d) if the airline loses their luggage?
e) if we forget our homework?
f) will the schools be closed?
g) if it's cold tomorrow?
h) what will happen to the garden?
i) will you hear it?
j) will I have more energy?

to wash   to iron   to polish   to hang   to make   to scrub

B. Choose the correct question word.

1. If we don't do our homework, (what/how) will anyone know?
2. (Who/How) will know if we are late for class?
3. (What/Where) will you do if you run out of money?
4. If the teacher is absent, (what/who) will correct our homework?
5. If we don't have bus tickets, (where/how) will we get home?
6. (When/What) will we study, if we go to a movie tonight?
7. (Where/How) will we get to class, if it snows tomorrow?
8. If it rains, (what/where) will we have the picnic?
9. (What/Who) will teach the class, if the teacher is sick?
10. If it's cold tomorrow, (what/how) will we wear?

UNDERSTAND: **Indefinite Pronouns**

Use an indefinite pronoun to refer to a person, thing, or place without being specific. Pronouns that end with **one** or **body** refer to people, and have the same meaning. The indefinite pronoun **no one** is written as two words.

Use a **singular** verb form with indefinite pronoun subjects:

Somebody is at the door.

No one is home.

Look at the chart of indefinite pronouns.

everyone	someone	anyone	no one
everybody	somebody	anybody	nobody
everything	something	anything	nothing
everywhere	somewhere	anywhere	nowhere

Use **everyone/everybody** or **everything** to refer to all members of a group:

Everyone (Anne, Keiko, Max, and our other friends) is here now.

Everything (the music, the food, etc.) is ready for the party.

Use **someone/somebody** or **something** in affirmative statements or in questions when you expect a positive response.

Someone (I don't know who) ate the last piece of cake.

Would you like **something** (juice, water, coffee, etc.) to drink?

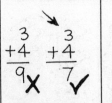   

to correct　　a cake　　a pie　　an ice cream　　cookies　　a chocolate bar

Use **anyone/anybody** or **anything** to underline a non-specific possibility. Use **any-** in negative statements or questions:

> **Anyone** you ask (the public, friends, etc.) knows that sharks are dangerous.
>
> The witness didn't see **anything**.
>
> Did **anyone** remember to buy milk?

Use **no one/nobody** or **nothing** to refer to the absence of a person or thing. Do not use these pronouns if the verb is negative. Use **anyone** or **anything** after the verb.

> ✗ He didn't say nothing.
>
> ✔ He said nothing.
>
> ✔ He didn't say anything.

> I telephoned the lawyer's office but **nobody** (not the receptionist, not the lawyer, not the secretary, etc.) answered.
>
> The doctor said that **nothing** (not a cold, not the 'flu, etc.) was wrong with me.
>
> **No one** (not your friends, not your teachers, etc.) understands you better than your mother.

A. Choose the correct indefinite pronoun to complete the sentences.

1. My glasses are lost. I can't find them (anywhere/somewhere).

2. (Someone/Anyone) is ringing the doorbell. Can you answer it please?

3. I looked (somewhere/everywhere) for my keys, but I couldn't find them.

4. I'm really hungry now. I didn't have (something/anything) for lunch.

5. It's my birthday tomorrow. Let's go (somewhere/anywhere) special for supper.

6. We had a great time last night. (Anyone/Everyone) we know was there.

7. I was waiting for a letter to arrive today, but there was (something/nothing) in the mail.

8. Did (anyone/anything) remember to buy stamps?

9. I really liked the movie, but (everyone/no one) agreed with me.

10. Thanks for helping me carry those heavy bags. Just put them (anywhere/anything).

| a shark | a witness | mail | stamps | a letter | a doorbell |

B. Some sentences have errors with indefinite pronouns or subject/verb agreement. Find the errors and correct them.

1. I went to the store but they didn't have nothing I wanted.
2. She called everyone to see if they had the book she needed.
3. I didn't see no one at the park this afternoon.
4. Did you ask anyone for help with your homework?
5. Everyone were at the party last weekend.
6. I asked for help but anybody helped me.
7. Nobody were at home when I dropped by this morning.
8. Were there anything in the envelope?
9. I ate the leftover spaghetti for supper. There wasn't nothing else in the fridge.
10. I called one store, but they didn't have the tape I wanted. Maybe I can try somewhere else.

Language in Transition

In formal English, pronouns and possessive adjectives that refer to indefinite pronouns are singular:
> Someone (a man) forgot his coat.
> Someone (a woman) forgot her coat.

In spoken English, however, it is more common to use plural pronouns to include the possibility of he or she:
> Someone forgot their coat.

UNDERSTAND: **"Else" with Indefinite Pronouns**

Use the word **else** after a possessive pronoun to underline the idea that there is an indefinite alternative.

> This beach is too crowded. Let's go somewhere **else**.

Match the two parts of the conversation.

1. There is too much noise here. I can't hear you.
2. The telephone keeps ringing. I can't get any work done.
3. I'm a vegetarian so I can't eat meat.
4. This restaurant is very crowded.
5. Max can't help with the moving on Saturday.
6. I feel silly wearing a hat, gloves, and heavy boots.

a park   crowded   spaghetti   boots   gloves   a meal

7. We have worked on this project too long. Let's stop now.

8. This subject is getting boring.

9. I didn't understand the teacher's explanation.

10. The sun is shining directly in my eyes.

a) Never mind. We can ask someone else to help us.

b) Don't worry. If anyone else calls, I'll take a message.

c) I agree. I can't think of anything else to add.

d) Why don't we go somewhere else to talk?

e) Why don't you ask someone else to explain it?

f) Well, we can always eat somewhere else.

g) If you don't want meat you can order something else.

h) You won't be alone. Everyone else will be wearing them too.

i) It's in my eyes too. Let's find chairs somewhere else.

j) Okay. Why don't we talk about something else?

Listening and Speaking: Using Idioms

Can You Pick Up a Few Things?

A. Choose the appropriate idiomatic expression to substitute for the words in bold type.

1. When you go to the pharmacy, can you **pick up** some soap?
   a) lift up
   b) buy
   c) choose

2. I'm going to be **on the run** all day. I have a lot of things to do.
   a) running quickly
   b) running away from someone
   c) doing things quickly

3. We are **out of** cereal. We should go to the store and buy some.
   a) have none left
   b) are outside
   c) have a few

a message

cereal

soap

toothpaste

dental floss

slippery

4. It's raining today. When you drive to work, **keep in mind** that the roads are slippery.
   a) be careful
   b) remember
   c) hold

5. My plane leaves at 3:00. It's almost 2:00 now, so I'm **running short of** time.
   a) don't have much left
   b) am moving quickly
   c) am moving slowly

6. When you leave the house, **make sure** to lock the door.
   a) be certain
   b) be worried
   c) try not

7. We have to plan the party for next week. Let's **make out** a list of things to do.
   a) draw
   b) think about
   c) prepare

8. I don't have many things to do today, so we can **take our time** and have a nice lunch.
   a) go quickly
   b) go slowly
   c) look at your watch

9. Tomorrow is a holiday. We should **take advantage of** the time off to visit our friends.
   a) be in a good place
   b) benefit from
   c) take it from someone

10. Toothpaste is on sale at the pharmacy. We should **stock up on** the kind we like.
    a) buy a large quantity
    b) make a large pile
    c) put it in a box

B. Listen and answer the questions.

1. Why does Harry have a problem buying the food?
2. What does June ask him to buy?
3. Why does Harry want to go shopping the next day?
4. What do June and Harry want to take advantage of?

Turn to page 200 for Exercise C.

a razor blades shaving cream deodorant a shower cap tweezers

Ten-Minute Grammar Games

Sentence Ends

Focus: Practise indefinite pronouns.

Students work in pairs to complete these sentences. They use as much imagination as they can. Then they take turns reading their sentences to the class.

1. Everyone in the class would be very happy if…
2. No one in the class wants to…
3. Somebody in the class…
4. Did anybody in the class…?
5. Everybody in the world knows that…
6. Nothing in this room is…
7. Something near the window is…
8. Everything we need is…
9. Does anyone have…?
10. Someone in the class forgot to…

Chains

Focus: Practise conditional sentences.

This can be done as a whole class activity or in groups. It can be done orally or as a story written by partners or a small group.

One student begins a sentence with an **if** clause. The second person adds on to the second part of the clause, and so on. Students continue the chain for as long as possible.

> If I win a million dollars in the lottery, I will get a fancy new car. If I get a new car, I will take a long trip. If I take a long trip, I will…

Sayings and Superstitions

Focus: Practise conditional sentences.

Many sayings and superstitions begin with if clauses:

> If you find a four-leaf clover, you will have good luck.

> If you spill salt, throw some over your shoulder, or you will have bad luck.

Students work in a group. They list as many sayings and superstitions as they can. Then they compare their list with another group.

Test Yourself

Conditional Sentences

A. Put the verbs in the correct tense. Choose the negative or affirmative form to be logical.

1. If there is no wind, a kite _____ (fly).
2. If you don't eat breakfast, you _____ (be hungry).
3. You _____ (be cold) if you forget your coat today.
4. Many people _____ (be late) for work today if there is a bus strike.
5. If you lose your wallet, you _____ (have) any money.

6. We _____ (watch) the movie tonight if we finish our work on time.

7. If you help me with my work, I _____ (finish) on time.

8. If this picture is nice, I _____ (send) it to your grandmother.

9. I _____ (have) enough food for supper if I don't go to the store right now.

10. If the weather doesn't warm up, we _____ (go) to the park.

B. Some sentences have errors. Find errors in the verb tenses and correct them.

1. If she doesn't answer the phone, she'll know who called.

2. You won't get better if you don't go to the doctor.

3. If I save enough money, I buy a car next year.

4. If my printer doesn't work, I won't print the document.

5. No one will answer the phone if the secretary was late.

6. She won't finish her sentence if you interrupts her.

7. He doesn't go to the party if he is sick tomorrow.

8. The lamp won't work if the light bulb is burned out.

9. The children won't go to sleep if their mother don't kiss them good-night.

10. I won't call you tonight if I are too tired.

C. Put the verbs in the correct tense.

1. If you don't go, everyone _____ (be) sad.

2. The party will be a success if everyone _____ (come).

3. Max won't serve meat, if you _____ (be) vegetarian.

4. If you work hard, you _____ (pass) the exam.

5. If Susan hears the bell, she _____ (answer) the door.

6. If Jack and Jean are late again, I _____ (say) something.

7. We won't have the exam, if anybody _____ (be) absent.

8. Gaby will let us know if she _____ (get) an answer.

9. If the phone rings, someone _____ (hear) it.

10. If Mei doesn't understand me, I _____ (speak) more slowly.

Indefinite Pronouns

Complete the sentences.

1. I can't find my homework assignment _____.

2. _____ called and left a message for you.

3. We can smell the cooking _____ in the house.

4. Janet didn't know _____ at the party last night.

5. _____ wants to play tennis. I guess I'll stay home.

6. Jun put his car keys _____ but he can't remember where.

7. There is _____ you should know before you decide.

8. _____ has a better climate than Costa Rica.

9. _____ will make Fred change his mind about football.

10. She didn't want to go _____ alone in a new city.

200

Idioms

Use idioms to complete the paragraph. Use the correct form of the expressions below to help you.

to pick up
to be on the run
to be out of something
to keep in mind
to run short of

to make sure
to make out
to take one's time
to take advantage of
to stock up

Buying on Sale

A good way to save money is to shop when stores are having sales. _____ in mind that most stores have regular sales, so by checking the newspaper, you can take _____ of the low prices and _____ up on items you use every day. You can certainly save money by making sure you don't run _____ of things you need. Sometimes you realize that you are _____ of something on a day when you are on the _____. Then you have to make a special trip to _____ up what you need.

It's a good idea to take your _____ to make _____ a list of things you need every week. Then, to save money, make _____ you buy things when they are on sale.

Score for Test Yourself: _____
50

Listening and Speaking: Using Idioms

Can You Pick Up a Few Things?

C. Listen and write the missing words.

June: If you have time today Harry, can you pick _____ a few things at the supermarket?

Harry: I'll try June, but I'll be on the _____ all day. What do you need?

June: Well, we're out _____ milk and bread.

Harry: I'll keep it in _____. Anything else?

June: We're also running short _____ fruit. Maybe you can pick up some bananas. Make _____ you don't get green ones. Oh, and some apples….

Harry: It sounds like you need more than a few things. If you make _____ a list, I can go tomorrow when I'm not in a rush. Then I can take my _____ and get everything you need.

June: That's a good idea. We can take advantage _____ the weekend specials and stock _____ on a few things we need.

D. Practise the dialogue with a partner.

E. Work with a partner. Write a new dialogue about shopping for groceries. Use as many idioms as you can.

15 Review Unit

The "What If" Quiz

Put the verbs in the correct tense. Then choose the best ending for each statement.

1. An ambulance _____ (use) its siren
   a) if the weather is bad.
   b) if it is in a hurry.
   c) if the driver is late.

2. If there _____ (be) an accident,
   a) people will call the fire department.
   b) everyone will go back to work.
   c) someone will call the police.

3. If you _____ (not study) hard,
   a) you will see the exam.
   b) you won't pass the exam.
   c) you will pass the exam.

4. If I _____ (want) to sell my car,
   a) I will read an ad in the paper.
   b) I will see an ad in the paper.
   c) I will put an ad in the paper.

5. Dinner _____ (be) ready soon,
   a) if some people are hungry.
   b) if everyone helps cook it.
   c) if nobody arrives late.

6. We _____ (cancel) our plans for a picnic
   a) if it doesn't rain.
   b) if the weather is bad.
   c) if it's a sunny day.

7. If I _____ (not receive) a letter soon,
   a) I will be worried.
   b) I won't buy any stamps.
   c) I will try to write more often.

8. If you _____ (want to) apply for the job,
   a) you won't need an application form.
   b) you will take a vacation next week.
   c) you will need letters of reference.

9. People _____ (not go) to the beach,
   a) if they are on holiday.
   b) if it is a cold day.
   c) if they can swim there.

10. If the new photocopy machine _____ (break down),
    a) we will make copies for everyone.
    b) we won't need any more copies.
    c) we will use the old machine.

Reactions

A. Match the pictures a-j with the sentences on page 205.

1. Lili has just locked her keys in her office.
2. Franco has just dropped some papers on the floor.
3. Mario has just turned off the photocopier.
4. Mr. Tan and Mr. Smith have just been introduced.
5. Maria has just put on her coat.
6. Max has dropped a filing cabinet on his foot.
7. Lee has decided to lose some weight.
8. Julie and Carol have just noticed that it is noon.
9. Tom has just noticed that his chair is broken.
10. Someone has rung the fire alarm.

B. Look at the pictures again and decide what is going to happen next. Match the reaction to the picture.

k) He is going to shout with pain.
l) She is probably going to go home.
m) He isn't going to make any more photocopies.
n) She is going to call security to let her in.
o) He isn't going to eat much for lunch.
p) They are going to go for lunch.
q) He is going to bend over and pick them up.
r) The fire department is going to come.
s) They are going to shake hands.
t) He is not going to sit on it.

Irregular Past Participles

Use these clues to complete the puzzle.

Across

4. Have you _____ a letter to your mother this week?
6. That woman has _____ her keys.
7. You haven't _____ that sweater for ages.
10. Have you ever _____ that movie?
11. Someone has _____ all of the coffee.
12. I haven't _____ my fall courses yet.
15. I haven't _____ to any of my friends yet today.

Down

1. I've already _____ my homework to the teacher.
2. How long have you _____ Rosalie?
3. He has never _____ a car before.
5. I've _____ a lot of pictures with this camera.
8. Have you ever _____ a horse?
9. How long have you _____ here?
13. Have you ever _____ in this restaurant before?
14. Where have they _____ on holiday?
15. We have already _____ "Happy Birthday" three times today.

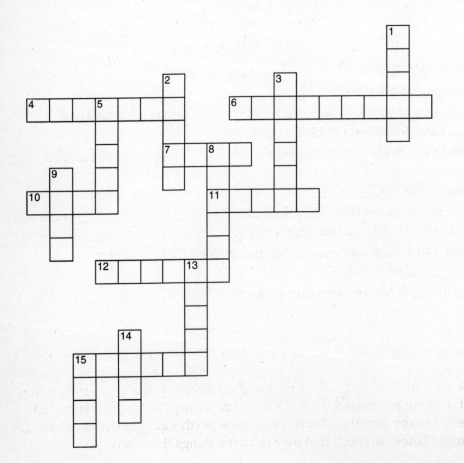

Making Conversation

Read the stories. Then complete the dialogues with the words that are suggested.

Story A

Janet and Jill have been neighbours for several years. It was Jill's birthday last week and Janet decided to surprise her with a birthday cake. She bought the best ingredients and, because she knew how much Jill liked chocolate, she made a chocolate cake. She called Jill and asked her to come over for coffee. When Jill rang the doorbell, Janet lit the candles so the cake would be ready. Jill was very surprised and happy. The two friends sat down and ate a piece of cake. Then they ate another piece, and another. Soon they had eaten the whole cake.

1. **something, anything**

   Janet: Hi Jill. It's Janet. Are you doing _____ right now?

   Jill: Hi Janet. How are you? No I'm not doing _____ at the moment, but I do have _____ to do later in the evening.

   Janet: Well, do you feel like coming over now for coffee and _____ to eat?

   Jill: Sure. It would be nice to see you. I'll be right over.

2. **something, anything, nothing**

   Janet: I'm coming. Just a minute.

   Jill: Hi Janet. _____ smells good. Have you been baking?

   Janet: Come into the living room. I have _____ to show you.

   Jill: What a lovely surprise! You didn't have to do _____ like this.

   Janet: Oh it's _____. Happy Birthday, Jill.

3. **something, anything, nothing**

   Jill: I didn't know you knew how to bake. This cake is delicious. I haven't had _____ this good for ages.

   Janet: Well, thank you. I'm glad you like the cake, but I didn't do _____ special.

   Jill: Are you sure? There is _____ special about the icing.

   Janet: Oh, I know. It's probably the Swiss chocolate. There's _____ better than Swiss chocolate. Would you like another piece?

   Jill: I can't resist. But I think we're eating too much. Soon there won't be _____ left.

   Janet: I think you're right. We've eaten the whole cake. There's _____ left.

Story B

Fred and Frank are planning a fishing trip at a lake about 100 kilometres from the city. They will be away for several days so they have to be careful to take enough supplies with them. Fred offers to look after the fishing licence, fishing gear, and maps. Frank offers to look after the food and cooking equipment they will need for the trip. Before they leave they have to check carefully to be sure they haven't forgotten anything. They decide to meet at Fred's house the night before to check that they have the things they need.

1. **everything, nowhere, anything, nothing**

   Fred: Hi Frank. Thanks for coming over. I think it's important to be sure we haven't forgotten _____.

   Frank: I agree. I'm sure we have _____ but it's always good to check.

   Fred: It would be terrible to be stuck in the woods and discover we had _____ to eat.

   Frank: No problem. I went to the supermarket and got _____ on the list.

   Fred: Good, because there is _____ to buy food at the lake.

2. **something, anything, nothing**

   Frank: I hope you brought _____ to read. It can get boring in the evening.

   Fred: Oh, I'm glad you reminded me. I didn't pack _____ to read. I'll pick up _____ before we leave.

   Frank: Don't forget. I'll go crazy if I have _____ to read.

   Fred: By the way, do you like detective stories?

   Frank: Sure. I'm not fussy. I like _____ that's easy to read and that has a lot of action.

3. **nowhere, somewhere, anywhere, everywhere**

   Frank: Do you have a map so we won't get lost?

   Fred: Yes I have a map _____ in this box.

   Frank: Let's look at the map. Wow! The lake is really in the middle of _____.

   Fred: Yes. All we are going to see is trees _____ we look.

   Frank: Let's keep the map _____ near us. I don't want to get lost.

   Fred: Don't worry, Frank. We won't go _____ dangerous.

Appendix 1: Spelling

Spelling Verb Forms Ending "ing"

The spelling rules for continuous verbs are different from the rules for regular past tense verbs. For example, with the verb **try**, the past tense is **tried**, but the continuous tense is **trying**.

Rule 1   Verbs that end with **e** drop the **e** and add **ing**:

    write   writing

Rule 2   Verbs that end with two consonants (**n,d,k, b**, etc.) or with two vowels (**a,e,i,o,u**) add **ing**:

    try   trying
    read   reading

Rule 3   Verbs that end with a vowel and a consonant double the final letter and add **ing**:

    put   putting

    Exceptions: consonants **w, x**, and **y**. (**buy**   **buying**)

Note: Verbs that end **ie** change the **i** to **y** and add **ing**:

    die   dying
    lie   lying

Spelling Simple Past Tense

2 consonants	add **ed**	work	work**ed**
2 vowels + consonant	add **ed**	need	need**ed**
vowel + **y**	add **ed**	play	play**ed**
consonant + **y**	change **y** to **i** add **ed**	try	tried
vowel + consonant	double consonant add **ed**	plan	plan**ned**

Not all verbs that end in vowel + consonant double the final letter. Common exceptions are **listened, opened, answered**.

For pronunciation rules see *Grammar Connections 1*.

Spelling Rules with Comparative Forms

Adjectives that end in **y** change **y** to **i** and add **er** for the comparative or **est** for the superlative form:

happy	happier
silly	silliest

Adjectives that end in vowel + consonant double the final letter and add **er** for the comparative or **est** for the superlative form:

fat	fatter
thin	thinner

Spelling Plural Nouns

Nouns that end in **s, ch, sh, z, o** add **es** to form the plural:

watch	watches
box	boxes
potato	potatoes

Nouns that end in consonant + **y** change the **y** to **i** and add **es** for the plural form:

city	cities
activity	activities

Nouns that end in vowel + **y** add s:

day	days
key	keys

Nouns that end in **f** or **fe** change the **f** to **v** and add **es** to form the plural:

leaf	leaves
knife	knives

Irregular Plurals

person	people
child	children
woman	women
man	men
mouse	mice
foot	feet
tooth	teeth
ox	oxen

Appendix 2: Past Participles

Many past participles are the same as the regular or irregular past tense forms. Irregular past participles are shown in bold type below.

Present	Past	Past participle
arise	arose	**arisen**
awake	awoke	**awaken**
be	was, were	**been**
beat	beat	**beaten**
become	became	**become**
begin	began	**begun**
bite	bit	**bitten**
bleed	bled	bled
blow	blew	**blown**
break	broke	**broken**
bring	brought	brought
build	built	built
buy	bought	bought
catch	caught	caught
choose	chose	**chosen**
come	came	**come**
cost	cost	cost
cut	cut	cut
dig	dug	dug
do	did	**done**
draw	drew	**drawn**
drink	drank	**drunk**
drive	drove	**driven**
eat	ate	**eaten**
fall	fell	**fallen**
feed	fed	fed
feel	felt	felt
find	found	found

Present	Past	Past participle
fly	flew	**flown**
forbid	forbade	**forbidden**
forget	forgot	**forgotten**
forgive	forgave	**forgiven**
freeze	froze	**frozen**
get	got	**gotten** (got)
give	gave	**given**
go	went	**gone**
grow	grew	**grown**
have	had	had
hear	heard	heard
hide	hid	**hidden**
hit	hit	hit
hold	held	held
hurt	hurt	hurt
keep	kept	kept
know	knew	**known**
lay	laid	laid
lead	led	led
leave	left	left
let	let	let
lie	lay	**lain**
lose	lost	lost
make	made	made
mean	meant	meant
meet	met	met
pay	paid	paid
put	put	put

Present	Past	Past participle
read	read	read
ride	rode	**ridden**
ring	rang	**rung**
rise	rose	**risen**
run	ran	**run**
see	saw	**seen**
sell	sold	sold
send	sent	sent
shake	shook	**shaken**
shine	shone	shone
shoot	shot	shot
show	showed	shown
shrink	shrank	**shrunk**
shut	shut	shut
sing	sang	**sung**
sit	sat	sat
sleep	slept	slept
speak	spoke	**spoken**

Present	Past	Past participle
spread	spread	spread
spring	sprang	**sprung**
stand	stood	stood
steal	stole	**stolen**
stink	stank	**stunk**
swear	swore	**sworn**
swim	swam	**swum**
take	took	taken
teach	taught	taught
tear	tore	**torn**
tell	told	told
think	thought	thought
throw	threw	**thrown**
understand	understood	understood
wake	woke	**woken**
wear	wore	**worn**
win	won	won
write	wrote	**written**

Appendix 3: Modals for Different Functions

Modal Auxiliary Verbs

Ability **can, be able to**

> I can play tennis.
> I am able to swim.

Permission **can, could, may, might**

> You can go now.
> Could I use your pen?
> May I be excused?
> Might I invite her?

Polite requests **can, could, would you**

> Can you help me?
> Could you pass that?
> Would you open the door?

Offering, promising, agreeing, refusing **will**

> I'll get it.
> I'll try to come.
> I won't be there.

Necessity **must, have to**

> I have to go now.
> I must leave at once.

Obligation **should, have to, must**

> I should study more.
> I have to work hard.
> I must get good marks.

Lack of Necessity **to not have to**

> I don't have to study.

Appendix 4: Special Verb Forms, Special Questions

Special Verb Forms

used to + verb	habitual past	I used to be a student.
to be going to	future time	I am going to study hard.

Special Questions

How much	for quantity	How much water is there?
How many	for number	How many apples are there?
How long	for distance	How long is the trip?
	for time	How long did you wait?
How big	for size	How big is your car?
How often	for times	How often do you exercise?
How heavy	for weight	How heavy was the package?

Index

Test Yourself Answers

Unit 1

Present Time

A. (Page 13)

1. Karen works in an office downtown.
2. She usually leaves for work early because she likes to arrive early.
3. She doesn't have time for coffee when she is late.
4. She likes to read the newspaper before she starts her job.
5. She begins work at 9:00.
6. Fred sometimes arrives in a bad mood because he has trouble finding a place to park his car.
7. He often has to park several blocks away.
8. Karen lives near the subway.
9. Karen is happy about where she lives because she doesn't have to worry about parking.
10. Maxine and Lili walk to work.

B. (Page 13)

1.	b	6.	b
2.	a	7.	a
3.	b	8.	b
4.	a	9.	a
5.	a	10.	b

Questions (Page 14)

1. Where does Min work?
2. When does she work?
3. Why does she like her job?
4. Where is she working today?
5. What is she making?
6. Who does she call when the sandwiches are ready?
7. Where does the server carry the sandwiches?
8. What is the customer ordering?
9. Where is Min making the coffee?
10. Why are Min and the server tired?

Negative (Page 14)

1. The bus company doesn't have 50 buses on the road.
2. The buses don't serve all the people in the city.
3. Tony doesn't drive a bus on the weekends.
4. Tony isn't working for the bus company at the moment.
5. He doesn't want to drive a bus all his life.
6. Susanna isn't learning Tony's route.
7. She doesn't want to work during the week.
8. They don't like to work at night.
9. The bus company doesn't ask her to work on Sundays.
10. Susanna isn't thinking about getting a new job.

Idioms (Page 15)

I take the bus to work almost every day. I **get on** the bus at the corner of my street. My neighbour, Kathy, sometimes takes the bus too. She also works downtown. Sometimes we **bump into** each other at the bus stop. My friend Joe often **gets on** the bus there too. He works at a hospital, so he **gets off** at the bus stop near the front door of the hospital.

On some mornings there isn't much traffic, and we get downtown **in no time**. We **get off** the bus near our offices. Kathy sometimes drives to work, so she **gives** me a **lift**. She **picks** me **up** at my house, and we drive down together. Then Kathy parks her car in the parking lot behind her building. Kathy works with two people who live in our neighbourhood. When she **bumps into** them in the corridor, she offers to **give** them a **lift** home.

Unit 2

Indefinite Articles

A. (Page 28)

Tom and Louise are moving to **a** new house. They need many things for their kitchen. They need **a** stove with **an** oven. They also need **a** refrigerator and **a** washing machine. Tom wants **a** table and **some** folding chairs.

Louise and Tom love their back yard. They need many things there too. They need **a** table, **some** chairs, and **an** umbrella for the patio. Louise wants to plant **some** vegetables near the fence. She wants to plant **some** tomatoes and **some** carrots. Tom likes fruit trees. He wants to have **an** apple tree in the yard.

Louise and Tom have children. They have **a** young girl and **an** older boy. The children have **some** pets. They have **a** small cat, **an** enormous dog, and **some** (**a**) fish. They are happy because there is **a** big yard to play in. They want to meet **some** children from the neighbourhood and play in the back yard.

B. (Page 28)

1. Some
2. 0
3. Some
4. 0
5. 0
6. Some
7. Some
8. 0
9. Some
10. 0

Definite Articles (Page 29)

1. The temperature in this city can be very high.
2. Many people in North America have pets.
3. Correct
4. Most households have telephones.
5. Correct
6. The police station is down the street.
7. A lot of people in Vancouver work in offices.
8. The traffic lights at the corner are not working.
9. Correct
10. Correct

Idioms (Page 29)

1. grab it
2. for the time being
3. close to
4. all right
5. opens up
6. for good
7. kept her eyes open
8. right

Unit 3

Simple Past Tense

A. (Page 44)

Give ½ point per answer.

bring	brought
catch	**caught**
come	**came**
drink	drank
drive	**drove**
eat	ate
find	**found**
get	got
go	**went**
hear	**heard**
make	made
put	**put**
ring	**rang**
run	ran
sit	sat
stand	**stood**
take	**took**
throw	threw
wake	**woke**
win	won

B. (Page 45)

Give ½ point per answer.

Carla: I really enjoyed that holiday. The guide **told** us such interesting stories.

Roberto: He didn't **tell** interesting stories. He **told** boring stories.

Carla: Well anyway, the weather was great. We **swam** in the ocean and **walked** on the beach every day.

Roberto: We didn't **swim** in the ocean and **walk** on the beach every day. We **swam** in the ocean twice, and we walked on the beach once.

Carla: Yes well… We were lucky. We **had** a fabulous hotel room with a magnificent view of the mountains.

Roberto: We didn't **have** a fabulous hotel room. We **had** a small, hot, stuffy hotel room. And we didn't even **see** the mountains. We **saw** a few hills.

Carla: Well, the entertainment was really good. The woman who **sang** opera was excellent, and the people who **danced** ballet were very good too.

Roberto: Actually, the entertainment wasn't that good. The singer was okay, but she didn't **sing** that well. By the way, the people didn't **dance** ballet, they danced jazz.

Carla: Well, we ate some delicious food. The chef **prepared** some wonderful new dishes.

Roberto: The chef didn't **prepare** new dishes. He **prepared** some very spicy dishes.

Carla: Oh, I give up. You tell the story, Roberto!

C. (Page 46)

1. didn't send
2. wrote
3. brought
4. didn't speak
5. stole
6. didn't want
7. didn't see
8. understood
9. lost
10. didn't tell

"Used to" (Page 46)

1. used to go
2. still wears
3. used to live
4. used to find
5. used to practise
6. still smokes
7. used to enjoy
8. used to do
9. used to play
10. still speak

Idioms (Page 47)

Last month, my sister Maria moved to another city to study English. At **first** I really **missed** her a lot. Of course I still think about her, but at **least** I don't think about her all **the time** now.

When she arrived, she wrote me a letter **right away** to say that she **missed** me, but that she had a chance to **make friends** in her English class. She said that she and her new friends **have fun** together on the weekends. Sometimes she goes to the movies or **takes a walk** with her friends. She is lucky to live in a small town because people are not usually in **a hurry**.

Unit 4

Comparison of Adjectives

A. (Page 60)

1. the **most** famous
2. is **newer**
3. is the **largest**
4. a **healthier**
5. Is it **better**
6. the **moodiest**
7. The **least** interesting
8. the **most** popular
9. the **fattest** athletes
10. the **best** form

B. (Page 61)

1. prettier
2. worst
3. easiest
4. bigger
5. farther
6. luckiest
7. slimmer
8. dirtier
9. wider
10. youngest

C. (Page 61)

1. Muscles Plus
2. the YMCA
3. the YMCA
4. Joe's Gym
5. the YMCA
6. Muscles Plus
7. Joe's Gym
8. Joe's Gym
9. Joe's Gym
10. Muscles Plus

"One" and "Ones" (Page 61)

1. the one
2. the fat ones
3. the ones
4. the short one
5. Correct
6. Correct
7. one is/ones are
8. Correct
9. the one
10. which one is/which ones are

Idioms (Page 62)

1. would rather
2. what's on
3. switch over to
4. make up my mind
5. can't stand
6. guess so
7. turn on, turn off
8. for a while
9. tired of

Unit 6

"Should" to Give Advice

A. (Page 83)

1. You should study.
2. She shouldn't come to class.
3. He should take an aspirin.
4. They should try to relax.
5. You shouldn't go swimming.
6. You shouldn't have dessert.
7. We should take an umbrella.
8. You should cook a good dinner.
9. You should clean it up.
10. They shouldn't expect to pass.

B. (Page 83)

1. shouldn't go
2. has to do
3. Correct
4. Correct
5. should eat
6. mustn't stand
7. should drive
8. don't have to
9. shouldn't go
10. mustn't forget

Polite Requests

A. (Page 83)

1. a
2. a
3. b
4. b
5. a
6. a
7. b
8. a
9. b
10. a

B. (Page 84)

1. Could/Can you
2. Could/would/can you
3. Correct
4. Could/can/may I
5. Correct
6. Correct
7. Correct
8. Correct
9. could/can/may I
10. Correct

Idioms (Page 84)

1. by now
2. slow down
3. under the weather

4. take it easy
5. a check-up
6. get better
7. be catching
8. come down with something
9. feel better
10. What's the matter?

Unit 7

Past Continuous (Page 99)

The Football Game

You should have been there! It was a huge crowd. People in front **were jumping** up and down. One man had a camera. He **was taking** pictures. Someone else **was selling** peanuts. We **were sitting** in the back row. A lady near us **was using** binoculars. The teenagers in front of us **were holding** up a sign.

It was exciting to be there with all that action. Our team **was running** all over the field. Player 36, Player 16, and Player 19 **were passing** the ball. The crowd **was cheering** wildly. Suddenly I looked down and the ball **was flying** between the goalposts. What a great game!

B. (Page 99)

1. wasn't raining	6. was taking
2. Correct	7. weren't shopping
3. were sitting	8. were cheering
4. Correct	9. were eating
5. Correct	10. weren't checking

C. (Page 99)

1. when	6. while
2. While	7. While
3. When	8. While
4. While	9. When
5. while	10. when

"Another," "Other," "Others" (Page 100)

Man:	Excuse me. I left my raincoat on the plane. Do you have a raincoat there?
Airport Agent:	Which airline? Was it Air Canada?
Man:	No, it was **another** airline. It was KLM.
Airport Agent:	Were you on KLM 867 this morning?
Man:	No, it was one of their **other** flights.
Airport Agent:	Was it Flight 536 this afternoon?
Man:	Maybe, or maybe it was **another** one. Did you find a raincoat?
Airport Agent:	Yes, I have a blue raincoat here.
Man:	Do you have some **others**? My coat is tan.
Airport Agent:	We have a tan coat. It's size 46.
Man:	That's not mine. Do you have **other** sizes?
Airport Agent:	Yes, we have some **others**. What size is your coat?
Man:	It's size 40.
Airport Agent:	I have a 40 in blue. Oh wait, here are some **other** ones.
Man:	What do the **other** ones look like?
Airport Agent:	One's smaller than the **others**. It's size 38.
Man:	Yes, I think that one is mine. Can I come and get it today, or is **another** day better?
Airport Agent:	No sir, come today. If it's not one of these coats, I'm sure it's **another** one.

Idioms (Page 100)

1. 5:00 sharp
2. go off
3. get through to
4. just one of those things
5. Never mind
6. give me a minute
7. take off
8. get through to
9. take off

Unit 8

"How much"/"How many"

A. (Page 114)

1. many	6. much
2. much	7. much
3. much	8. many
4. many	9. much
5. much	10. many

Quantifiers

A. (Page 115)

1. many	6. much
2. a lot of	7. Correct
3. much	8. Correct
4. a lot of	9. Correct
5. much	10. many

B. (Page 115)

1. a few	6. a little
2. a few	7. few
3. a little	8. a few
4. few	9. a little
5. little	10. a few

C. (Page 115)

1.	no	6.	none of
2.	None of	7.	no
3.	none	8.	none
4.	None of	9.	no
5.	no	10.	no

Idioms (Page 116)

Mauricio is taking a trip to Paris this summer. The summer is a good time to travel because Mauricio has **time** off from his classes. He **booked** his ticket last week. At first, the travel agent suggested a **package** deal because it was less expensive that way, but Mauricio wanted to **talk** it over with his family.

Finally Mauricio decided to buy a **one-way** ticket, because he wasn't sure how long he would stay. He knew that he could always get a **return** ticket later. He asked the travel agent to **make** out the ticket for June 15, because he wanted to **pick up** the ticket early. Mauricio's friend called to ask for information about the trip. Mauricio told her that he would find out if there were still tickets available, and would get **back to** her right away. He suggested that if she wanted to go, she should also **book** her ticket early.

Unit 9

Gerunds

A. (Page 127)

1.	Raising	6.	Doing
2.	Overeating	7.	smoking
3.	swimming	8.	Sitting
4.	camping	9.	jogging
5.	Walking	10.	Exercising

B. (Page 128)

1.	swimming	6.	Arriving
2.	Correct	7.	eating
3.	Eating	8.	Correct
4.	Smoking	9.	riding
5.	Correct	10.	skating

C. (Page 128)

1.	before	6.	at
2.	in	7.	to
3.	about	8.	after
4.	of	9.	from
5.	for	10.	over

Reflexive Pronouns (Page 128)

1.	himself	6.	ourselves
2.	Correct	7.	yourselves
3.	Correct	8.	himself
4.	themselves	9.	Correct
5.	Correct	10.	Correct

Idioms (Page 129)

1. good at
2. as usual
3. Quite a few
4. made a difference
5. introduce yourself
6. help yourself
7. make yourself
8. introduced myself; quite a few
9. as usual

Unit 11

Present Perfect Aspect for Duration of Time

A. (Page 149)

1.	was	6.	had
2.	has worked	7.	have known
3.	has lived	8.	worked
4.	went	9.	spoke
5.	has lived	10.	has been

B. (Page 150)

1. She's been sick for 3 days.
2. She's been in the waiting room for 20 minutes.
3. He's had a sore throat for 2 days.
4. They've been home from school all week.
5. She's had this fever for 24 hours.
6. She's been off work for 5 days.
7. She's had 3 headaches this week.
8. They've been married for 6 months.
9. He's had a cough for 6 days.
10. He's had a sore neck for 2 days.

C. (Page 150)

Answer according to the time, day, and date it is now.

1. It has been cold for _____ days.
2. We have been here for _____ hours.
3. Joe has worked here for _____ months.
4. Paul has spoken English for 6 months.
5. Sue and Bob have known each other for _____ years.
6. Keiko has had a cold for _____ days.
7. My brother has been at university for _____ years.
8. They have lived next door to us for _____ years.
9. I have spoken English for _____ months.
10. Mike has worked in China for _____ years.

"Everyone," "Everything," "All," "Every," "Both" (Page 150)

1.	everyone	6.	every
2.	Every	7.	both
3.	all	8.	all
4.	Both	9.	All
5.	All	10.	everything

Idioms (Page 151)

1. take your pick
2. can't afford, look for
3. look around
4. look for
5. they have in mind
6. am at a total loss
7. next door
8. too good to be true
9. hold on/hold it

Unit 12

Present Perfect Aspect for Indefinite Past Time

A. (Page 166)

1. has learned
2. drove
3. visited
4. has eaten
5. worked
6. has gone
7. have been
8. made
9. have fallen
10. have spoken

B. (Page 166)

1. Correct
2. have never gone
3. have never met
4. ever eaten
5. Correct
6. Correct
7. has never studied
8. has never been
9. Correct
10. has never been

C. (Page 166)

Ben: This is a wonderful hotel. Have you **ever** stayed here before?

Jerry: No, **never**, but Ellen has stayed here a few times. She has **already** booked it for her next trip.

Ben: I hear they have a great swimming pool. Have you tried the swimming pool **yet**?

Jerry: No, not **yet**. I want to eat something first. Do you want to join me?

Ben: Sure. I know a good restaurant. Have you **ever** eaten Japanese food? This place has great sushi.

Jerry: I've eaten Japanese food, but I've **never** eaten sushi.

Ben: I've **already** made reservations for seven o'clock. It isn't seven o'clock **yet**.

Jerry: We haven't tried the pool **yet**. Let's take a swim and then go for dinner.

Ben: Great idea. Then when we arrive at the restaurant, we'll **already** have a good appetite.

Intensifiers (Page 167)

1. too
2. too
3. too
4. very
5. very
6. too
7. very
8. too
9. too
10. very

Idioms (Page 167)

Monica and Victor have just bought a house. The house is old, and it's in pretty bad **shape**, but Monica and Victor are not worried because they plan to **fix** it up. They know that they can't do everything **at** once. That would be **out** of the question, since they don't have a lot of money right now. **So** far they have painted three rooms, and they have got **rid** of some old wallpaper in the bathroom. The kitchen counter is old and **worn** out too, but that is too expensive to repair, so they will have to make the **best** of it for a while.

For now, they will **put** away all their dishes and cutlery. Then they will begin to fix **up** the kitchen a little at a time.

Unit 13

Future with "Will"

A. (Page 183)

1. will get
2. will phone
3. will join
4. will ask
5. will take
6. will leave
7. will meet
8. will empty
9. will beep
10. will tell

B. (Page 183)

1. won't
2. will
3. will
4. won't
5. won't
6. will
7. will
8. won't
9. will
10. won't

Future with "Be going to" (Page 183)

1. am not going to come
2. is going to end
3. is going to work
4. are not going to meet
5. is going to buy
6. Correct
7. are going to take
8. is not going to be
9. going to get together
10. Correct

Future with Present Tenses (Page 184)

1. When does Dan's plane get in?
2. Where does the monthly meeting take place?
3. Why is Sylvia leaving early on Tuesday?
4. When is the repairman coming?
5. What time does the switchboard open on Monday?
6. Where is Dan meeting his boss?
7. What is he bringing with him to the office?
8. When is Janice taking her holidays this year?
9. When does she leave for Paris and Barcelona?
10. Who is replacing her in the office when she leaves?

Idioms (Page 184)

1. on the dot
2. will take place
3. will you get in
4. fill me in
5. go over it
6. carry on, get here
7. make it
8. had better
9. fill me in

Unit 14

Conditional Sentences

A. (Page 198)

1. won't fly
2. will be hungry
3. will be cold
4. will be late
5. won't have
6. will watch
7. will finish
8. will send
9. won't have
10. won't go

B. (Page 199)

1. she won't know
2. Correct
3. will buy
4. Correct
5. is late
6. interrupt
7. won't go
8. Correct
9. doesn't kiss
10. am too tired

C. (Page 199)

1. will be
2. comes
3. are
4. will pass
5. will answer
6. I will say
7. is
8. gets
9. will hear
10. will speak

Indefinite Pronouns (Page 199)

1. anywhere
2. Somebody/Someone
3. everywhere
4. anybody/anyone
5. Nobody/No one
6. somewhere
7. something
8. Nowhere
9. Nothing
10. anywhere

Idioms (Page 200)

A good way to save money is to shop when stores are having sales. **Keep** in mind that most stores have regular sales, so by checking the newspaper, you can take **advantage** of the low prices and **stock** up on items you use every day. You can certainly save money by making sure you don't run **short** of things you need. Sometimes you realize that you are **out** of something on a day when you are on the **run**. Then you have to make a special trip to **pick** up what you need.

It's a good idea to take your **time** to make **out** a list of things you need every week. Then, to save money, make **sure** you buy things when they are on sale.

Answer Key

Unit 1

Word Power (Page 2)

1. T	6. F
2. T	7. F
3. T	8. F
4. F	9. T
5. T	10. T

Understand: Present Simple Tense

Affirmative (Page 4)

1. No, it rises in the east.
2. Yes, they do.
3. No, they go by different means of transportation.
4. No, he goes to work by car.
5. No, she walks to the bus stop.
6. No, she takes the bus to work.
7. No, she walks to the bus stop a few blocks away.
8. No, she lives in an apartment.
9. Yes, she does.
10. No, she doesn't. She goes to class by subway in winter.

Negative (Page 5)

1. In the summer I don't drive to work.
2. It doesn't take a long time to get downtown.
3. The subway doesn't open at six o'clock.
4. Mei and Karen don't leave for work at the same time.
5. Vancouver and Kyoto don't have subway systems.
6. Bob doesn't go to work by public transportation.
7. Miguel doesn't like to walk to work.
8. Suzanne and Tania don't live in the same building.
9. The bus doesn't leave at exactly 8:15.
10. Mike doesn't ride his bike to class in the winter.

Question (Page 6)

1. Does	6. like
2. Correct	7. drive
3. Do	8. take
4. Correct	9. need
5. Correct	10. ride

Understand: Present Continuous Tense

A. (Page 7)

This is a picture of Mother's Day at my house. My mother **is sitting** at the table. She **is reading** the newspaper. My father is at the stove. He **is cooking** some eggs. My younger sister **is putting** flowers on the table. They are a surprise for mother. My older brother **is standing** at the counter. He **is pouring** coffee into two mugs. I am at the counter too. I **am making** toast. I **am waiting** for the toast to be ready. My older sister **is holding** a package. It is a Mother's Day present. We **are having** a good time.

B. (Page 8)

take	listen
study	walk
learn	speak
look at	give
eat	read
sit	

C. (Page 8)

Students write their own answers with these verbs.

taking	listening
studying	walking
learning	speaking
looking at	giving
eating	reading
sitting	

Negative (Page 9)

1. Ray isn't taking the bus today.
2. The sun isn't shining this morning.
3. They aren't listening to music in the living room.
4. Maurice isn't learning to speak Japanese.
5. My neighbours aren't travelling in South America.
6. The students aren't writing an exam now.
7. Yumi isn't giving Max a birthday gift.
8. It isn't raining hard right now.
9. She isn't reading an exciting novel in her English class.
10. They aren't watching a movie on the TV.

Question (Page 9)

1. Correct
2. Correct
3. taking
4. Correct
5. waiting
6. looking
7. Correct
8. waiting
9. reading
10. Correct

Understand: Present Simple and Present Continuous in Contrast

A. (Page 10)

Susan **works** downtown. Usually she **drives** her car to work. This morning she is in the subway. She **is looking** at her watch. She **likes** to arrive for work on time.

Tony usually **walks** to work. Today he **is taking** the bus. A lot of people **are standing** at the bus stop. It **is raining**. People **are holding** up their umbrellas. Tony **wants** to go home and sleep.

B. (Page 10)

1. Correct
2. He walks
3. Correct
4. They like
5. Correct
6. Correct
7. He often brings
8. He likes
9. he is reading
10. Correct

Do You Want a Lift Sometime?

B. (Page 11)

1. to enter a vehicle
2. to leave a vehicle
3. to meet by accident
4. to give someone a ride in a car
5. to get someone and give them a ride
6. very soon

C. (Page 11)

1. by bus
2. She gets off the 49, and gets on the 103 bus.
3. She drives.
4. at the bus stop

D.

Ana:	How do you usually come to class, Nancy?
Nancy:	I take the bus. How about you, Ana?
Ana:	I usually take the bus too. Which bus do you take?
Nancy:	I take the 49 to Berry Street. I get off at Berry Street, and get on the 103. That takes me right downtown.
Ana:	Oh. I take the 56. I also get **off** at Berry Street and **get** on the 103.
Nancy:	Really? Well, maybe we'll bump **into** each other some time on the bus.
Ana:	Sure. Anything's possible. Sometimes I drive to work though. Do you want a **lift** some time?
Nancy:	That would be great. If you pick me **up** at the bus stop, we can get downtown in **no** time.

Solve the Problem (Page 12)

Michiko	=	Decorator
Maria	=	Journalist
Gaby	=	Model

Unit 2

Understand: Indefinite Articles

Singular Count Nouns (Page 20)

1. a hospital
2. an hour
3. an ambulance
4. a hardware store
5. a bench
6. a store
7. a university
8. a fire hydrant
9. a police officer
10. an opera singer
11. an honest man
12. a neighbour
13. an accident
14. a garden
15. an avenue
16. a street
17. an open window
18. an elevator
19. an indoor pool
20. an umbrella

Plural Count Nouns (Page 20)

1. taxis
2. mailboxes
3. skyscrapers
4. traffic lights
5. cross walks
6. libraries
7. subways
8. ambulances
9. hospitals
10. parks

Indefinite Quantities (Page 21)

1. Some flowers smell nice.
2. Ice is cold.
3. Grass is green./Some grass is green. (Some is yellow).
4. Fish swim.
5. Some neighbours are friendly.

6. Some fire trucks are yellow.
7. Some cats don't like water.
8. Some buses are air-conditioned.
9. Some parties are fun.
10. Some students work hard.
11. Some sugar is white.
12. Candy is sweet.
13. Some cities are dirty.
14. Some children are noisy.
15. Tropical countries are hot.
16. Some men are handsome.

Non-count Nouns (Page 22)

Count nouns	Non-count nouns
a flower	water
a store	air
a hospital	garbage
an orderly	gas
a car	police
a telephone	mail
a neighbour	fun
a fence	sunshine
an ambulance	
a fire fighter	
a letter carrier	
a park	
a child	

Understand: Definite Articles

A. (Page 23)

(Possible answer types)
1. in the picture, who have blue eyes
2. that grow in the garden, with long stems
3. in the bathtub, that I drank
4. on the corner, where I was born
5. who is talking, with the moustache
6. where we ate, with the terrace
7. about modern art, that you gave me
8. near my house, with a lot of trees
9. in the driveway, that you admired
10. that you drank, on the table

B. (Page 23)

1. 0
2. 0
3. the
4. 0
5. The
6. The
7. the
8. The
9. 0
10. the
11. the
12. 0
13. 0
14. the
15. the

My Neighbourhood

A. (Page 24)

1. b
2. a
3. b
4. a
5. a
6. b
7. b
8. b

B. (Page 25)

1. downtown
2. It's close to his work.
3. There's a lot of traffic and it's noisy.
4. a place in a quiet neighbourhood

C. (Page 29)

Carlos: Where do you live, Mario?
Mario: I live **right** downtown, Carlos.
Carlos: Do you like it?
Mario: Yeah, it's all **right** for the time **being**, because it's close **to** my work.
Carlos: That sounds good.
Mario: It is. But there's a lot of traffic on my street, and it's noisy. It's okay for now, but I'm not staying here for **good**.
Carlos: I understand. I live in a busy part of town too, but I'm keeping my eyes **open** for a place in a quieter neighbourhood. If something good opens **up**, I'll grab **it**.
Mario: Well, good luck.
Carlos: You too.

What Are They? (Page 26)

Unit 3

Understand: Simple Past Tense

A. (Page 34)

1.	l	10.	j
2.	o	11.	d
3.	m	12.	r
4.	c	13.	q
5.	b	14.	a
6.	g	15.	n
7.	p	16.	h
8.	f	17.	e
9.	k	18.	i

B. (Page 35)

When we were young, we **lived** in the country. My brother and I **went** to school together every day. We often **met** our friends along the road. We usually **took** our time. We **hunted** rabbits and looked for fruit trees. The road to the school **ran** past farmers' fields.

One fall day we **got** into trouble with a farmer. We **found** an apple tree. When we **saw** the juicy red apples, my friend **climbed** the tree. He picked apples and **threw** them down. I **caught** the apples and we all **ate** a lot. The farmer **saw** us eating his apples and was very angry.

We **brought** a nice red apple to the teacher at school. My brother **put** the apple on the teacher's desk. When the teacher **saw** the apple, she said, "Thank you." Nobody **told** her where the apple **came** from.

C. (Page 36)

1.	came	6.	met
2.	brought	7.	told
3.	put	8.	knew
4.	threw	9.	took
5.	ate	10.	ran

Understand: Simple Past Tense Negative Form

A. (Page 37)

1.	h	9.	l
2.	o	10.	d
3.	g	11.	a
4.	j	12.	f
5.	m	13.	k
6.	e	14.	b
7.	c	15.	i
8.	n		

B. (Page 37)

1. The bus driver **didn't drive** dangerously.
2. The passengers **didn't sit** at the front of the bus.
3. The driver **didn't know** all the passengers.
4. We **didn't sing** quiet songs during the bus ride.
5. He **didn't see** a person running after the bus.
6. The driver **didn't speak** to the man behind him.
7. They **didn't wait** in the rain for half an hour.
8. You **didn't ride** your bicycle to work every day last year.
9. We **didn't hear** the siren of a police car.
10. The driver **didn't wear** a uniform with a hat.
11. She **didn't ring** the bell three times.
12. The old lady **didn't stand** for the whole ride.
13. The driver **didn't make** a mistake and **have** an accident.
14. We **didn't leave** before the five o'clock rush hour.
15. We **didn't get off** at the last bus stop.

C. (Page 38)

1.	didn't **ride**	6.	didn't **try**
2.	Correct	7.	Correct
3.	didn't **wear**	8.	didn't **want**
4.	didn't **see**	9.	didn't **speak**
5.	didn't **understand**	10.	Correct

Understand: Simple Past Tense Question Form

A. (Page 38)

1.	k	9.	i
2.	m	10.	d
3.	l	11.	c
4.	j	12.	e
5.	n	13.	h
6.	o	14.	f
7.	g	15.	b
8.	a		

B. (Page 39)

1. What did Ben win?
2. Where did Ben spend last summer?
3. What did he love?
4. Why did he usually wake up early?
5. Where did he go for breakfast?
6. What did he usually have?
7. Where did Ben always sit?
8. What did he order?
9. What did he read?
10. When did Ben pay the bill?

C. (Page 39)

1.	Where did you **go**	6.	Where did she **sit**
2.	Why did you **leave**	7.	Did Jennifer **spend**
3.	Did you **watch**	8.	did you **pay**
4.	Did everyone **drink**	9.	did they **feel**
5.	did you **wake up**	10.	did they **win**

228

Understand: "Used to" + Verb

D. (Page 41)

1. **F** Pablo is a university student now.
2. **F** He is busier now.
3. **T**
4. **T**
5. **F** He can only see them on the weekend.
6. **T**
7. **F** He had to stop to pay attention to his studies.
8. **F** He used to have more free time than he has now.
9. **F** He doesn't go to concerts and movies anymore.
10. **T**

A New Country

A. (Page 42)

1. b   6. c
2. c   7. c
3. b   8. b
4. a   9. b
5. a

B. (Page 43)

1. took a language course
2. take long walks all the time
3. her old friends
4. in her English class

C. (Page 47)

Maria: How do you feel here, Li? Do you **miss** your country?
Li: Well, I did at **first**, Maria. I took a language course right **away**, so I learned to speak English. At **least** I can communicate.
Maria: Do you miss the things you used to do in your country?
Li: Yes. I used to **take** long walks all the **time**. Here, everyone is in a **hurry**. I never go for a walk.
Maria: What do you miss the most?
Li: I **miss** my old friends.
Maria: Well, you met some nice people in your English class.
Li: Yes. I **made** some new friends, and we have a lot of **fun** together.

Solve the Problem (Page 43)

1. He took the duck, leaving the dog and the grain.
2. He took the dog, leaving the grain, and then came back with the duck.
3. He took the grain, leaving the duck.
4. He went back for the duck.

Unit 4

Understand: Comparative Form of Adjectives

A. (Page 52)

1. older
2. more satisfying (less satisfying)
3. harder
4. less dangerous
5. fatter
6. less tasty (more tasty/tastier)
7. less unusual
8. more enjoyable
9. warmer
10. more efficient

B. (Page 52)

1. Walking is less exhausting than running.
2. Running in a race is more challenging than running alone.
3. Figure skaters are less violent than boxers.
4. Basketball players are taller than runners.
5. Football players are less graceful than divers.
6. Baseball is slower than soccer.
7. Sprinters are faster than distance runners.
8. Skiing is more expensive than jogging.
9. Golf is less (more) exciting than tennis.
10. Hockey is rougher than baseball.

Understand: Comparisons with "As" + Adjective + "As"

A. (Page 53)

1. not as easy as   6. not as rough as
2. as expensive as   7. as graceful as
3. as tall as   8. not as cheap as
4. not as fast as   9. not as rich as
5. not as interesting as 10. as violent as

Understand: Superlative Form of Adjectives

A. (Page 54)

1. the youngest   6. the strongest
2. the least tired   7. the tallest
3. the fastest   8. the most skillful
4. the happiest   9. the most talented
5. the most graceful 10. the most courageous

B. (Page 54)

1. b   6. d
2. g   7. c
3. a   8. i
4. f   9. e
5. h

Understand: Question Word "Which"

A. (Page 55)

1. Which game do you watch?
2. Which team does he prefer?
3. Which foods do they eat?
4. Which friends do you invite?
5. Which day does she go?
6. Which sport does Jim like best?
7. Which pool does Sharon go to?
8. Which team does he play for?
9. Which player does he like best?
10. Which league does Helen compete in?

B. (Page 55)

1. Which day do you play soccer?
2. Which coach does he study with?
3. Correct
4. Correct
5. Which county does she represent?
6. Which tennis racket does he use?
7. Correct
8. Correct
9. Which skates do you like?
10. Which season do you play in?

Understand: Pronouns "One" and "Ones" (Page 56)

1.	e	6.	a
2.	c	7.	b
3.	k	8.	d, l
4.	m, n	9.	j
5.	l	10.	h

What's On?

B. (Page 58)

1.	d	6.	g
2.	i	7.	e
3.	j	8.	b
4.	a	9.	f
5.	h	10.	c

C. (Page 58)

1. watching TV
2. a tennis match
3. the tennis match is boring
4. baseball
5. soccer
6. (turn off the TV), listen to music on the radio

D. (Page 62)

Ali: What do you want to do tonight, Bob? Do you want to watch TV?

Bob: I'm not sure, Ali. Let's turn **on** the TV and see what's **on**.

Ali: Hey, there's a tennis match on Channel 13. Let's watch for a **while**.

Bob: Nah, it's boring. Let's **switch** over to Channel 16 and see if there's a game on.

Ali: Okay. I think the baseball game is on Channel 16.

Bob: I'm tired **of** watching baseball.

Ali: Would you **rather** watch the soccer game?

Bob: No, I can't **stand** soccer.

Ali: Do you want to watch TV, or not? Make up your **mind**.

Bob: I guess **not**. Let's turn **off** the TV and listen to music on the radio.

Unit 5

Old Friends (Page 63)

Lisa: Hi, Marco. What are you doing here? I **thought** you didn't like parties.

Marco: Hi, Lisa. How are you doing? You **have** a good memory. I didn't used to like parties, but I **like** this one.

Lisa: What are you **doing** these days? Are you still studying psychology?

Marco: No, I **graduated** last June. Now I'm working as a school counsellor. What are you up to these days?

Lisa: I'm still **trying** to finish my degree. I **am taking** my last three courses this semester. Tell me about your job. It sounds interesting.

Marco: I **enjoy** it a lot because I **learn** a lot of new things every day.

Lisa: What kind of things do you do?

Marco: I meet students to advise them about courses or help them with personal problems. I really like working with young people.

Lisa: Well, it's nice to **see** you again. Good luck with your new job.

The Bus Strike (Page 64)

Last year there was **a** bus strike in Winnipeg. The first day of **the** bus strike was the **coldest** day of the year. The second day we had the **worst** snow storm of the century. **The** snow storm caused **a** power failure and some parts of the city had no electricity or heating for three days. **The** people who normally **rode** the bus had to find other ways to get to their jobs. **Some** people used car pools and others **took** taxis. **The** lucky ones stayed home and waited for **the** storm to end. This was really a strike to remember!

Who Is Doing What? (Page 64)

(Possible answer types)

1. A man is getting into a taxi.
2. A woman is walking a dog.
3. A girl is running.
4. A boy is going into the subway.
5. A police officer is stopping traffic.

230

6. A man is working at a computer.
7. A woman is looking out the window.
8. A man and woman are waving to each other.
9. A man is delivering boxes.
10. A woman is holding a baby.

World Records Quiz (Page 65)

1. a
2. b
3. c
4. a
5. b
6. a
7. c
8. c

Irregular Past Tense Verbs (Page 67)

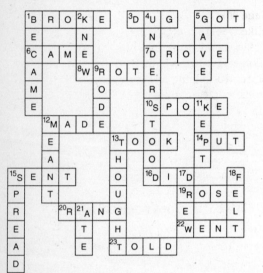

Unit 6

Understand: Giving Advice Using "Should" and "Must"

Should

A. (Page 72)

1. e
2. g
3. b
4. a
5. h
6. j
7. c
8. d
9. i
10. f

B. (Page 72)
(Possible answer types)

1. You should eat.
2. You shouldn't go out tomorrow./You should dress warmly.
3. We should stop smoking./You shouldn't smoke.
4. You should move to a colder climate.
5. You shouldn't take a taxi./You should take a bus.
6. You shouldn't go to see it./You should go to another movie.

7. You shouldn't ski anymore./You should relax and rest.
8. You shouldn't read in poor light./You should get a good lamp.
9. You should go to the Rockies to ski./You shouldn't go to the Adirondacks.
10. You should go to resorts where you can sit around the fire.

Must

A. (Page 73)

1. mustn't
2. must
3. mustn't
4. must
5. must
6. must
7. mustn't
8. mustn't
9. must
10. mustn't

B. (Page 74)

1. j
2. g
3. i
4. d
5. e
6. a
7. f
8. b
9. h
10. c

Understand: Obligation Using "Have to"

A. (Page 76)

1. d
2. f
3. a
4. j
5. e
6. c
7. h
8. i
9. g
10. b

B. (Page 76)

1. have to
2. has to
3. has to
4. have to
5. have to
6. have to
7. has to
8. have to
9. have to
10. has to

Understand: Prohibition and Lack of Necessity Using "Must not" and "Do not have to"

A. (Page 77)

1. mustn't
2. don't have to
3. don't have to
4. mustn't
5. doesn't have to
6. mustn't
7. doesn't have to
8. doesn't have to
9. don't have to
10. mustn't

B. (Page 78)

1. **doesn't** have to
2. **mustn't** take
3. Correct
4. Correct
5. **don't** have to
6. mustn't make
7. **don't** always have to
8. don't have **to** wait
9. Correct
10. **don't** have to

Understand: Using "Can," "Could," and "May" to Request Permission

A. (Page 79)

1.	come	6.	leave
2.	Correct	7.	Correct
3.	Can/Could	8.	Can/Could
4.	borrow	9.	Can we come
5.	Correct	10.	Correct

B. (Page 79)
(Possible answers)
1. May/Can/Could I use your dictionary?
2. May I please be excused?
3. Can/Could/May we leave class early?
4. May/Can/Could we smoke here?
5. May/Could I use your phone?
6. Can/Could my sister register for classes?
7. Can/Could he borrow your towel?
8. Can my friends stay here tonight?
9. May/Can/Could I sit here?
10. Can/Could I help you?

Understand: "Would," "Could," or "Can" for Polite Requests

A. (Page 80)

1.	Correct	6.	Correct
2.	Would **you**	7.	Can you **help**
3.	Could he **wait**	8.	Would **you**
4.	Correct	9.	**be** careful
5.	Correct	10.	Could he **try**

Under the Weather

A. (Page 80)

1.	a	5.	b
2.	a	6.	b
3.	b	7.	a
4.	a	8.	b

B. (Page 80)
1. She has a cold.
2. take it easy
3. make an appointment for a check-up

C. (Page 85)

Benito: What's the matter, Carla? You don't look well.

Carla: It's this cold. I **caught** it last week. I should **feel** better by **now**, but instead I feel **worse**.

Benito: Maybe you're working too hard. You should take **it** easy.

Carla: Yeah, I guess you're right. I really should take it **easy** when I'm feeling **under** the weather like this.

Benito: Do you think you're coming **down** with the 'flu? Maybe you should call the doctor.

Carla: Well, if I don't feel **better** tomorrow, I'll make an appointment for a **check-up**.

Unit 7

Understand: Past Continuous Tense

A. (Page 90)

1.	were making	6.	was carrying
2.	was raining	7.	were listening
3.	were sleeping	8.	were snoring
4.	were hurrying	9.	were studying
5.	was sitting	10.	was working

B. (Page 90)
1. Mike was studying.
2. Yuki was watching TV.
3. Leon was taking a bath.
4. Marta was talking on the phone.
5. Frank was exercising.
6. Maria was writing.
7. Nancy was washing her hair.
8. Walid was reading the newspaper.
9. Lili and Chen were playing chess.
10. Carla and Roberto were sleeping.

Understand: Past Continuous Negative

A. (Page 91)

1.	weren't trying	6.	weren't walking
2.	wasn't working	7.	wasn't looking
3.	wasn't driving	8.	wasn't trying
4.	weren't kicking	9.	weren't watching
5.	weren't running	10.	weren't shopping

B. (Page 92)

1.	f	4.	b
2.	d	5.	e
3.	c	6.	a

Understand: "When" and "While" with the Past Continuous and Simple Past

A. (Page 92)

1.	f	6.	g
2.	d	7.	j
3.	h	8.	a
4.	e	9.	i
5.	b	10.	c

B. (Page 93)

1.	e	6.	i
2.	j	7.	g
3.	c	8.	f
4.	a	9.	d
5.	b	10.	h

Understand: Adjectives "Another" and "Other" and Pronoun "Others"

A. (Page 94)

1. Another	6. other
2. another	7. another
3. Other	8. other
4. another	9. another
5. another	10. Other

B. (Page 94)

1. another	6. other
2. another	7. another
3. Others	8. another
4. Other	9. others
5. Others	10. Others

C. (Page 95)

1. other	6. Another
2. other	7. Correct
3. another	8. Correct
4. Correct	9. another
5. Others	10. Correct

What Happened to You?

A. (Page 95)

1. a	5. b
2. b	6. b
3. b	7. a
4. a	

B. (Page 95)

1. at 10:00
2. His alarm clock didn't go off.
3. The line was busy.
4. a lot of work

C. (Page 101)

Tom: You're really late today Max. What happened to you? We were supposed to meet at 10:00 **sharp**.

Max: I know, I know. I'm really sorry, Tom. My alarm didn't go **off**, so I slept in.

Tom: Why didn't you call?

Max: I called you, but I couldn't get **through**. The line was busy.

Tom: I know I was on the phone for a while, but it wasn't that long.

Max: Look, I said I was sorry. It's just one of those **things**.

Tom: Never **mind**. Let's get started. We have a lot of work to do today.

Max: Okay. Just give me a minute to take my coat **off**. Then we can get right to work.

What Were They Wearing? (Page 96)

	Ali	Maria	Ray	Alvaro	Junka
Course	Beginners	TOEFL	WW	Lab	Advanced
Sweater	red	yellow	black	blue	green

What Was Happening? (Page 97)

1. Two students were reading comics.
2. One student was sleeping.
3. Four students were playing cards.
4. One student was drawing a cartoon of the teacher on the board.
5. Two students were talking about their boyfriends.
6. One student was eating a sandwich.
7. One student was cutting their nails.
8. One student was listening to music on the tape.

Unit 8

Understand: "How Much"/"How Many"

A. (Page 105)

1. How many	6. How many
2. How much	7. How much
3. How many	8. How much
4. How many	9. How much
5. How many	10. How much

B. (Page 105)

1. many	6. Correct
2. Correct	7. many
3. Correct	8. many
4. many	9. much
5. much	10. many

Understand: Count and Non-count

A. (Page 106)

1. traffic	6. some water
2. information	7. trip
3. money	8. furniture
4. luggage	9. some good news
5. hair	10. any bread

B. (Page 106)

1. d	6. a
2. j	7. e
3. h	8. f
4. g	9. c
5. b	10. i

Understand: Quantifiers

"Much," "Many," "A lot of"

A. (Page 107)

1. a lot of
2. much
3. a lot of
4. a lot of
5. much
6. a lot of
7. many
8. a lot of
9. much
10. much

B. (Page 107)

1. not much
2. a lot
3. a lot
4. not much
5. not many
6. a lot
7. a lot
8. not many
9. not much
10. a lot

"Little"/"a little," "Few"/"a few"

A. (Page 108)

1. few
2. little
3. little
4. few
5. little
6. little
7. few
8. little
9. few
10. few

B. (Page 108)

1. a few
2. a little
3. a few
4. a few
5. a few
6. a little
7. a little
8. a few
9. a little
10. a few

"No," "None," "None of"

A. (Page 110)

1. There is no sunshine today.
2. There is no server for this part of the dining room.
3. There are no blue raincoats in the lost and found.
4. There are no frequent flyer points on this route.
5. There are no lifeguards on duty at the swimming pool.
6. There are no surfboards for rent at this resort.
7. There are no tour guides available today.
8. There is no discount on the price here.
9. There are no problems with our accommodations.
10. There are no plans to return.

B. (Page 110)

1. None of
2. no
3. none of
4. None of
5. none
6. no
7. None of
8. no
9. None of
10. no

A Package Deal

A. (Page 110)

1. b
2. c
3. a
4. b
5. b
6. a
7. b
8. b
9. c

B. (Page 112)

1. to Mexico
2. her friend
3. in April
4. She doesn't have any time off.
5. July is a busy month.
6. talk it over with her friend

C. (Page 116)

Travel Agent: Can I help you?

Woman: Yes, I'd like to go to Mexico on holiday. How much will it cost?

Travel Agent: That depends on what you want. Do you want a package **deal**?

Woman: No, I'm travelling with my friend. We don't want to travel in a group.

Travel Agent: Okay. Is that one **way** or return?

Woman: It's **return**. Do you have any specials?

Travel Agent: Yes, we have some special rates in April.

Woman: No, that's no good. I don't have any time **off** until the end of June.

Travel Agent: Well, July is a busy month. I suggest you **book** early. If you book this week I can make **out** the tickets, and you can pick them **up** next Friday.

Woman: Well, I'm not sure. I want to talk it **over** with my friend. When I make up my mind, I'll get **back** to you.

What Could It Be? (Page 113)

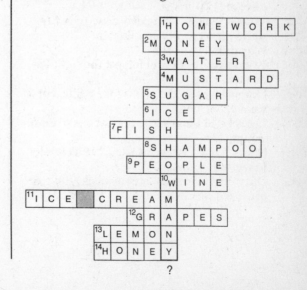

Numbers and Words (Page 114)

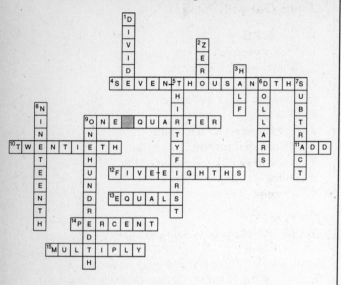

Unit 9

Understand: Gerunds

A (Page 119)

1. books d
2. exercise c
3. humour i
4. cigarettes h
5. weights e
6. silence g
7. ballet f
8. art b
9. rest a
10. TV j

B. (Page 120)

1. walking
2. smoking
3. jogging
4. breathing
5. exercising
6. getting
7. sunbathing
8. watching
9. eating
10. swimming, playing

C. (Page 120)

1. **of** shopping
2. **for** driving
3. **at** cooking
4. **about** forgetting
5. **in** playing
6. **about** seeing
7. **about** bringing
8. **without** saying
9. **without** wearing
10. **of** walking

Understand: Spelling the Gerund Form

A. (Page 121)

1. asking
2. swimming
3. playing
4. watching
5. sitting
6. stopping
7. running
8. forgetting
9. jogging
10. eating
11. trying
12. riding
13. shopping
14. planning
15. camping
16. smoking
17. skating
18. skiing
19. getting
20. hitting

B. (Page 121)

1. Correct
2. Sitting
3. riding
4. camping
5. jogging
6. swimming
7. Correct
8. stopping
9. Correct
10. Forgetting

Understand: Reflexive Pronouns

A. (Page 122)

1. themselves
2. ourselves
3. himself/herself
4. ourselves
5. itself
6. ourselves
7. herself
8. himself
9. yourself
10. yourselves

B. (Page 122)

1. myself
2. himself
3. themselves
4. itself
5. themselves
6. yourself
7. yourselves
8. herself
9. themselves
10. themselves

C. (Page 123)

1. by themselves
2. by myself
3. by yourself
4. by himself
5. by herself
6. by ourselves
7. by themselves
8. by yourself
9. by ourselves
10. by herself

Understand: Irregular Plural Forms

A. (Page 124)

1. spoons
2. knives
3. houses
4. children
5. husbands
6. wives
7. teeth
8. windows
9. lives
10. geese
11. animals
12. women
13. mice
14. leaves
15. forks
16. people
17. feet
18. halves
19. plates
20. thieves

B. (Page 124)

1. children
2. knives
3. mice
4. Correct
5. teeth
6. people
7. thieves
8. wives
9. Correct
10. Correct

Welcome to the Party

B. (Page 125)

1. c
2. g
3. f
4. e
5. d
6. b
7. a

C. (Page 125)
1. T
2. F
3. F (They made the food.)
4. T

D. (Page 129)
Lili: Hi Yumi. Welcome to the party. Come on in. Make **yourself** at home.

Yumi: Thanks Lili. Everything looks great. I always look forward to your parties.

Lili: Let me introduce you to some people.

Yumi: That's okay. I know **quite** a few people here. I can introduce **myself** to the others.

Lili: Okay. Please help **yourself** to some food.

Yumi: Did you and Chen make all this food **yourselves**?

Lili: Most of it. I made the main courses. Chen is very **good** at making desserts.

Yumi: Everything looks delicious, as **usual**. It really makes a **difference** when you prepare everything yourselves.

What Is It? (Page 126)

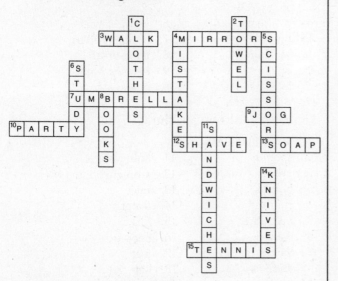

Bumping Words (Page 127)
eating
shopping
skating
asking
laughing
feeling

You will be definitely be **feeling** good when you finish this puzzle.

Unit 10
Dining Out with Fiona

A. (Page 131)
1. Friday evening
2. bread, water, the menu
3. ice in his water
4. some butter for her bread
5. poultry
6. The friend asked the waiter.
7. He didn't want any.
8. if she would like whipped cream
9. coffee
10. a receipt

B. (Page 132)
Diner 1: Could you (Would you) please come back later?

Diner 2: Could you (Would you) please give me a glass of water, and could you (would you) please put ice in it?

Diner 1: I would like (Could I please have) a green salad and roast duck. Please give me (Could you please give me) some butter with the bread.

Diner 2: Could I please have (Please give me) the fish soup and the Chicken Basquaise.

Server: Would you like any dessert?

Diner 2: No, thank you. I would just like some coffee.

Diner 1: I would like the chocolate mousse.

Server: Would you like whipped cream with the mousse?

Diner 1: Yes, please, and could you bring me some coffee too?

The Police Report

A. (Page 133)
1. Mr. Jones
2. three
3. the people at the bus stop
4. turning the corner
5. Mr. Black
6. five
7. sitting beside his car and holding his head
8. sitting in his truck
9. getting out of the car
10. calling an ambulance

The Doctor's Advice (Page 135)

1. **T**
2. **F** (Children under 12, elderly persons, pregnant or nursing women, and people with problems such as high blood pressure should not take it.)
3. **F** (It may cause drowsiness.)
4. **F** (Everyone should consult a physician if pain and fever persist.)
5. **F** (They can take a cold capsule very 12 hours.)
6. **T**
7. **T**
8. **F** (It is hazardous to exceed recommended dosage unless advised by a physician.)
9. **T**
10. **T**

Unit 11

Understand: Present Perfect Aspect for Duration of Time

A. (Page 140)

1. have been
2. has spoken
3. have worked
4. have gone
5. has been
6. has lived
7. has had
8. has worked
9. has known
10. has gone

B. (Page 141)

1. lived
2. has lived
3. has spoken
4. spoke
5. have been
6. has been
7. was
8. has known
9. knew
10. has had

Understand: "For" and "Since"

A. (Page 141)

1. for
2. since
3. since
4. for
5. since
6. since
7. for
8. for
9. for
10. since

B. (Page 142)

(Possible answer types)

1. ____ months, years
2. last February, 19__
3. ____ weeks, months, years
4. ____ weeks, months, years
5. 19__, they were children
6. yesterday, last week, Tuesday
7. 19__
8. ____ days, weeks, months, years
9. ____ months, years
10. yesterday, last week, Wednesday, last month

Understand: Present Perfect Questions Related to Duration of Time

A. (Page 142)

1. How long has Jun lived in Toronto?
2. How long has he gone to a technical college?
3. How long have Jun's uncle and aunt had a grocery store?
4. How long has Jun worked in the store on weekends?
5. How long has he known the young woman from New York?
6. How long have they been in the same classes?
7. How long has she spoken Korean?
8. How long has her family lived in New York?
9. How long has she worked in the library after school?
10. How long have Jun and the young woman been good friends?

B. (Page 143)

Interviewer: How long have you lived in Seattle?
Interviewee: I moved here 15 years ago.
Interviewer: Where do you work currently?
Interviewee: I work at Boeing in the engineering department.
Interviewer: How long have you worked there?
Interviewee: I've worked there for 10 years.
Interviewer: Have you always worked in the engineering department?
Interviewee: No I haven't.
Interviewer: How long have you worked in the engineering department?
Interviewee: For 3 years.

Understand: Present Perfect Negative Related to Duration of Time

A. (Page 144)

Number of Years Ago	Event
20	moved to Seattle
15	met Anita
12	got married
11	Anita got job at Boeing
10	Steve got job at Boeing
9	the Carters had a boy
7	the Carters had a girl, bought a car
8	the Carters bought a house

B. (Page 144)
(Possible answer types)

1. He hasn't lived in Seattle for 25 years. He's only lived in Seattle for 20 years.
2. He hasn't know Anita for 18 years. He's only known her for 15 years.
3. They haven't been married for 15 years. They've only been married for 12 years.
4. Anita hasn't worked for Boeing for 12 years. She's worked for Boeing for 11 years.
5. Steve hasn't worked for Boeing for longer than Anita has. He's only worked at Boeing for 10 years.
6. They haven't been parents for 12 years. They've only been parents for 9 years.
7. They haven't had a daughter longer than they have had a son. They've only had a daughter for 7 years.
8. They haven't had a car for 15 years. They've only had a car for 7 years.
9. They haven't lived in the suburbs for 10 years. They've only lived in the suburbs for 8 years.
10. They haven't been friends with their neighbours for 10 years. They've only been friends with their neighbours for 8 years.

Understand: "Everyone," "Everything," "All," "Every," "Both"

A. (Page 145)

1. both	6. Both
2. All	7. everyone
3. everyone	8. Both
4. All	9. everything
5. both	10. every

B. (Page 146)

1. every	6. every
2. all	7. both
3. both	8. everything
4. Every	9. all
5. Everyone	10. Everyone

At the Shopping Mall

A. (Page 147)

1. a	6. b
2. b	7. b
3. b	8. b
4. a	9. b
5. a	

B. (Page 148)

1. a birthday gift for a friend
2. Everything is overpriced.
3. sweaters
4. They are beautiful; The prices are too good to be true.

C. (Page 151)

Tina: I'm looking **for** a birthday present for a friend of mine. Do you have any ideas, Karen?

Karen: I don't know. What did you have in **mind**, Tina?

Tina: I'm not sure. I've known Julie for years, but I'm still at a total **loss** when it comes to buying her a gift.

Karen: Well, let's go into this store and look **around**. Wow! Everything is really overpriced here. Maybe we should try the store next **door**. I think they're having a sale.

Tina: That's okay by me. I don't think I can **afford** anything here.

Karen: Hold **on** a minute. Did you see these beautiful sweaters? They're actually on sale —half price!

Tina: Boy, we nearly missed those. These prices are too **good** to be true. I'm sure Julie would love one of these sweaters. And with these prices and this selection, I can take my **pick**.

Bumping Words (Page 148)

driven
spoken
brought
known
built
smiled
remembered

Good for you! You have **remembered** all the past participles!

Last Session (Page 149)

Room	#102	#104	#203	#206	# 207
Student	Ray	Tanya	Sophie	Anne	Gaby
Teacher	Grant	Jones	Koop	Shaw	Robb

Unit 12

Understand: Present Perfect Aspect for Indefinite Past Time

A. (Page 156)

1. has seen	6. have driven
2. have left	7. has gone
3. has written	8. have sung
4. has taken	9. have been
5. has made	10. has given

B. (Page 156)

1. took	6. spoke
2. visited	7. have written
3. wore	8. has eaten
4. learned	9. has begun
5. has drunk	10. knew

Understand: "Already," "Just," and "Yet" with the Present Perfect

A. (Page 157)

1. just	6. just
2. already	7. already
3. already	8. just
4. yet	9. already
5. yet	10. yet

B. (Page 159)

1. No, they haven't finished dinner yet.
2. Yes, they have eaten the fish already.
3. No, they haven't served coffee yet.
4. No, Lili hasn't blown out the candles yet.
5. No, she hasn't cut the birthday cake yet.
6. Yes, they have hung up the balloons.
7. No, they haven't washed the dishes yet.
8. No, she hasn't opened her presents yet.
9. No, they haven't sung Happy Birthday yet.
10. No, they haven't take a picture yet.

Understand: Present Perfect for Indefinite Past Time Negative

A. (Page 159)

1. haven't spoken	6. haven't begun
2. haven't done	7. haven't gone
3. hasn't taken	8. haven't met
4. hasn't drunk	9. hasn't seen
5. hasn't eaten	10. hasn't arrived

B. (Page 160)

2. He has never visited a foreign country.
4. He and his wife have never taken a plane.
8. He has never been to Las Vegas for the weekend.
9. Luc and his wife have never visited France.
10. He has never stayed home because of deep snow.

Understand: Present Perfect for Indefinite Past Time Questions

"Yet"

A. (Page 162)

1. c	6. g
2. h	7. d
3. b	8. a
4. f	9. e
5. i	10. j

Understand: Intensifiers

A. (Page 163)

1. too	6. very
2. very	7. too
3. very	8. too
4. too	9. too
5. very	10. too

B. (Page 163)

1. very	6. Correct
2. too	7. too
3. Correct	8. too
4. Correct	9. very
5. very	10. Correct

Moving In

A. (Page 163)

1. a	6. b
2. b	7. a
3. a	8. b
4. a	9. a
5. b	

B. (Page 164)

1. a week ago
2. a rug
3. as soon as she puts everything away
4. It was in bad shape.
5. It is worn out.
6. She can't afford to.
7. make the best of it

C. (Page 168)

Rita: Hi Margaret. How's your new apartment?

Margaret: Not bad, Rita. I just moved in a week ago, and I'm still unpacking boxes.

Rita: Have you got a lot of new furniture yet?

Margaret: Just a rug so **far**. As soon as I put everything **away** I'll start looking for the new things I need.

Rita: Didn't you have a lot of furniture in your old apartment?

Margaret: I did, but I had to get rid **of** a lot of things. Most of my furniture was in pretty bad **shape**.

Rita: Well, it will be nice when everything is fixed **up**.

Margaret: I know. I'm looking forward to that. The problem is that I can't afford to do everything at **once**. My sofa is really worn **out**, but buying a new one now is out of the **question**.

Rita: I know what you mean. I'd love to **fix** up my apartment too, but I don't have much money right now. I guess I'll just have to make the **best** of it.

Puzzles (Page 164)

1. the boy's mother
2. .25, .05 (One was not a quarter, but the other **was** a quarter.)

Participles (Page 165)

```
 ¹P A I D
 ²R U N
 ³E A T E N
 ⁴S E E N
⁵G O N E
  ⁶S U N G
   ⁷T A K E N
    ⁸P U T
⁹G I V E N
   ¹⁰D R U N K
     ¹¹F E L T
    ¹²B E C O M E
      ¹³C O M E
¹⁴W R I T T E N
      ?
```

The Old and the New (Page 165)

(Possible Answers)
1. The roof has already been fixed.
2. The fence has already been fixed.
3. The grass has already been cut.
4. The house has already been painted.
5. Flowers haven't been planted yet.
6. The bathroom hasn't been renovated yet.
7. The kitchen floor has already been fixed.
8. The kitchen already has a new stove.
9. The broken windows have already been fixed.
10. The windows already have curtains.

Unit 13

Understand: "Will" for Future Time (Page 172)

1. No, there won't.   6. No, she won't.
2. No, it won't.   7. No, he won't.
3. No, it won't.   8. No, it won't.
4. Yes, she will.   9. Yes, she will.
5. No, she won't.   10. Yes, she will.

Negative Form

A. (Page 173)
1. The meeting **won't be** in the boardroom today.
2. The meeting **won't be** over by three o'clock.
3. It **won't be** easy to get a dentist's appointment today.
4. John **won't tell** us what happened at the meeting.
5. She **won't be** out of the office all afternoon.

6. The new receptionist **won't remember** to turn off the coffee maker.
7. The photocopies of the forms **won't be** ready today.
8. The boss **won't interview** all the applicants tomorrow.
9. The decision **won't be made** this afternoon.
10. The office **won't be** open at eight o'clock.

Question Form

A. (Page 174)
1. e   6. g
2. h   7. a
3. b   8. d
4. f   9. i
5. j   10. c

B. (Page 174)
1. Shall   6. will
2. will   7. shall
3. will   8. will
4. will   9. Shall
5. shall   10. Shall

Understand: "Be going to" for Future Time

A. (Page 176)
1. She is going to take a taxi.
2. She is going to go to bed early on Sunday.
3. She is going to meet Joseph.
4. It is going to start at 8:30.
5. She is going to finish the report on Wednesday morning.
6. She is going to ask Louise to photocopy the report.
7. She is going to meet Anne for lunch on Tuesday.
8. She is going to attend the sales meeting on Friday.
9. She is going to work on the budget on Wednesday afternoon.
10. She is going to meet Susan in the board room.

B. (Page 176)
1. f. He is going to call security.
2. h. She is going to call the repairman.
3. i. She is going to get one from the coffee machine.
4. a. She is going to answer it.
5. j. He is going to ask his secretary to type it.
6. b. They are going to go outside to smoke.
7. d. She is going to go home and rest.
8. c. He is going to leave the office early.
9. e. They are going to take a taxi to work.
10. g. He is going to put in a rush order.

Negative Form (Page 177)

1. Correct
2. is not going to be
3. is not going to order
4. is not going to go/is not going
5. Correct
6. are not going to be
7. Correct
8. is going to call
9. is not going to smoke
10. is not going to ask

Question Form (Page 178)

1. When is the sales meeting going to be?
2. What are Marco and Tom going to arrange?
3. Where is Anne going to put flowers?
4. What are Kim and Frank going to distribute?
5. What is Gino going to do?
6. Who is going to order the food and beverages for the break?
7. How is the president going to open the meeting?
8. When is everyone going to arrive?
9. When is the meeting going to finish?
10. When are Jack and Steve going to clean up?

Understand: Using the Present Simple or Present Continuous for Future Time (Page 180)

1. are going
2. starts
3. are flying
4. lands
5. are staying
6. begins
7. are meeting
8. ends
9. are leaving
10. takes off

A Meeting

B. (Page 180)

1. b
2. d
3. f
4. g
5. c
6. h
7. a
8. e

C. (Page 181)

1. They have a lot of things to discuss.
2. at 3:00
3. Someone will give him the information (fill him in).
4. 2:00

D. (Page 185)

Alberto: Are you going to the meeting this afternoon, Kim?

Kim: Yeah, I think I'd **better**, Alberto. We have a lot to discuss. By the way, will Terry be at the meeting?

Alberto: I don't think so. His plane gets **in** at 3:00. I don't think he'll make **it** on time.

Kim: Oh well, we'll have to carry **on** without him. Someone will have to fill him **in** later.

Alberto: No problem. I can go **over** the information with him tomorrow.

Kim: Where will the meeting take **place**?

Alberto: In the board room. It starts at two on the **dot**.

Kim: Okay. See you there.

Solve the Problem (Page 182)

Ambassador from:	Mexico	Russia	Egypt	China
Airline	JAL	AF	Swiss	Singapore
Date	Jan 22	Dec 26	Feb 25	May 21
City	Istanbul	Paris	Ottawa	Tokyo

Unit 14

Understand: Conditional Sentences (Type I)

A. (Page 189)

1. j
2. i
3. e
4. h
5. b
6. c
7. g
8. d
9. f
10. a

B. (Page 189)

1. i
2. d
3. a
4. j
5. b
6. h
7. c
8. g
9. e
10. f

C. (Page 190)

1. rings, will answer
2. will call, breaks
3. will arrive, is
4. is, will do
5. comes, will get
6. will hire, improves
7. will order, ask
8. is, will put
9. will be, hear
10. collect, will save

D. (Page 191)

1. If you make
2. if we are lucky
3. If the exam is today
4. Correct
5. if they get home
6. if they cancel
7. Correct
8. If we go, we will have
9. Correct
10. if we cheat

Understand: Negation with Conditional I Sentences

A. (Page 191)
1. we won't go
2. I won't accept
3. The team won't win
4. My brother won't change jobs
5. I won't be late
6. they won't go to bed early
7. he won't stay up late
8. she won't carry it
9. The elevator won't work well
10. The car won't start easily

B. (Page 192)
1. b
2. b
3. a
4. a
5. b
6. a
7. a
8. b
9. a
10. b

Understand: Questions with Conditional I

A. (Page 192)
1. g
2. e
3. f
4. b
5. a
6. c
7. h
8. j
9. i
10. d

B. (Page 193)
1. how
2. Who
3. What
4. who
5. how
6. When
7. How
8. where
9. Who
10. what

Understand: Indefinite Pronouns

A. (Page 194)
1. anywhere
2. Someone
3. everywhere
4. anything
5. somewhere
6. Everyone
7. nothing
8. anyone
9. no one
10. anywhere

B. (Page 195)
1. anything
2. Correct
3. anyone
4. Correct
5. Everyone was
6. nobody
7. Nobody was
8. Was
9. anything
10. Correct

Understand: "Else" with Indefinite Pronouns

A. (Page 195)
1. d
2. b
3. g
4. f
5. a
6. h
7. c
8. j
9. e
10. i

Can You Pick Up a Few Things?

A. (Page 196)
1. b
2. c
3. a
4. b
5. a
6. a
7. c
8. b
9. b
10. a

B. (Page 197)
1. He'll be on the run all day.
2. milk, bread, and fruit
3. He won't be in a rush.
4. the weekend specials

C. (Page 200)

June: If you have time today Harry, can you pick **up** a few things at the supermarket?

Harry: I'll try June, but I'll be on the **run** all day. What do you need?

June: Well, we're out **of** milk and bread.

Harry: I'll keep it in **mind**. Anything else?

June: We're also running short **of** fruit. Maybe you can pick up some bananas. Make **sure** you don't get green ones. Oh, and some apples… .

Harry: It sounds like you need more than a few things. If you make **out** a list, I can go tomorrow when I'm not in a rush. Then I can take my **time** and get everything you need.

June: That's a good idea. We can take advantage **of** the weekend specials and stock **up** on a few things we need.

Unit 15

The "What If" Quiz (Page 203)
1. will use, b
2. is, c
3. don't study, b
4. want, c
5. will be, b
6. will cancel, b
7. don't receive, a
8. want to, c
9. won't like, b
10. breaks down, c

242

Reactions

A. (Page 205)

1.	e	6.	d
2.	f	7.	b
3.	a	8.	h
4.	i	9.	j
5.	c	10.	g

B. (Page 205)

a.	m	f.	q
b.	o	g.	r
c.	l	h.	p
d.	k	i.	s
e.	n	j.	t

Irregular Past Participles (Page 206)

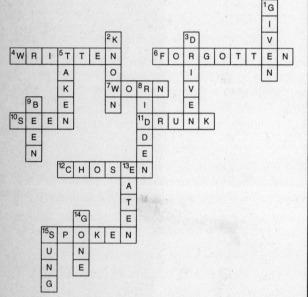

Making Conversation

Story A (Page 207)

1.

Janet: Hi Jill. It's Janet. Are you doing **anything** right now?

Jill: Hi Janet. How are you? No I'm not doing **anything** at the moment, but I do have **something** to do later in the evening.

Janet: Well, do you feel like coming over now for coffee and **something** to eat?

Jill: Sure. It would be nice to see you. I'll be right over.

2.

Janet: I'm coming. Just a minute.

Jill: Hi Janet. **Something** smells good. Have you been baking?

Janet: Come into the living room. I have **something** to show you.

Jill: What a lovely surprise! You didn't have to do **anything** like this.

Janet: Oh it's **nothing**. Happy Birthday, Jill.

3.

Jill: I didn't know you knew how to bake. This cake is delicious. I haven't had **anything** this good for ages.

Janet: Well, thank you. I'm glad you like the cake, but I didn't do **anything** special.

Jill: Are you sure? There is **something** special about the icing.

Janet: Oh, I know. It's probably the Swiss chocolate. There's **nothing** better than Swiss chocolate. Would you like another piece?

Jill: I can't resist. But I think we're eating too much. Soon there won't be **anything** left.

Janet: I think you're right. We've eaten the whole cake. There's **nothing** left!

Story B (Page 208)

1.

Fred: Hi Frank. Thanks for coming over. I think it's important to be sure we haven't forgotten **anything**.

Frank: I agree. I'm sure we have **everything** but it's always good to check.

Fred: It would be terrible to be stuck in the woods and discover we had **nothing** to eat.

Frank: No problem. I went to the supermarket and got **everything** on the list.

Fred: Good, because there is **nowhere** to buy food at the lake.

2.

Frank: I hope you brought **something** to read. It can get boring in the evening.

Fred: Oh, I'm glad you reminded me. I didn't pack **anything** to read. I'll pick up **something** before we leave.

Frank: Don't forget. I'll go crazy if I have **nothing** to read.

Fred: By the way, do you like detective stories?

Frank: Sure. I'm not fussy. I like **anything** that's easy to read and that has a lot of action.

3.

Frank: Do you have a map so we won't get lost?

Fred: Yes I have a map **somewhere** in this box.

Frank: Let's look at the map. Wow! The lake is really in the middle of **nowhere**.

Fred: Yes. All we are going to see is trees **everywhere** we look.

Frank: Let's keep the map **somewhere** near us. I don't want to get lost.

Fred: Don't worry, Frank. We won't go **anywhere** dangerous.